Up The Coast

Up The Coast

one family's wild life in the forests of British Columbia

Kathryn Willcock

NEWEST PRESS

EDMONTON, AB

Library and Archives Canada Cataloguing in Publication

Title: Up the coast : one family's wild life in the forests of British Columbia / Kathryn Willcock.
Names: Willcock, Kathryn, author.
Identifiers: Canadiana (print) 20210228288 | Canadiana (ebook) 20210228318 | ISBN 9781774390511 (softcover) | ISBN 9781774390528 (ebook)
Subjects: LCSH: Willcock, Kathryn. | LCSH: Willcock, Kathryn—Family. | LCSH: Loggers—British Columbia—Pacific Coast—Biography. | LCSH: Lumber camps—British Columbia—Pacific Coast—History—20th century. | LCSH: Forests and forestry—British Columbia—Pacific Coast—History—20th century. | LCSH: Pacific Coast (B.C.)—Biography. | LCGFT: Autobiographies. Classification: LCC SD537.52.W55 A3 2022 | DDC 634.9/8092—dc23

NeWest Press wishes to acknowledge that the land on which we operate is Treaty 6 territory and a traditional meeting ground and home for many Indigenous Peoples, including Cree, Saulteaux, Niitsitapi (Blackfoot), Métis, and Nakota Sioux.

Board Editor: Sandra Anderson
Cover painting: "Up the Coast" © 2016 Elizabeth Sutherland-Cox
Author photograph: Geoffrey Shuen
All Rights Reserved

NeWest Press acknowledges the Canada Council for the Arts, the Alberta Foundation for the Arts, and the Edmonton Arts Council for support of our publishing program. This project is funded in part by the Government of Canada.

201, 8540 – 109 Street
Edmonton, AB T6G 1E6
780.432.9427
www.newestpress.com

NEWEST PRESS

No bison were harmed in the making of this book.
PRINTED AND BOUND IN CANADA
1 2 3 4 5 24 23 22

For my family and the loggers of Bute Inlet

A ragged edge runs along one side of the map as if it had been ripped off the spine of an atlas. But this is not vandalism. This is the coast of British Columbia, twenty-five thousand kilometres of jagged inlets and jutting islands running hell-bent from the 49th parallel to the silence of places with names no white person has ever heard. Here, the mountains free-fall into the ocean, leaving no room for gentle terrain, and the trees along the shoreline stand crippled and twisted in the wind. This is serious beauty.

Bute Inlet

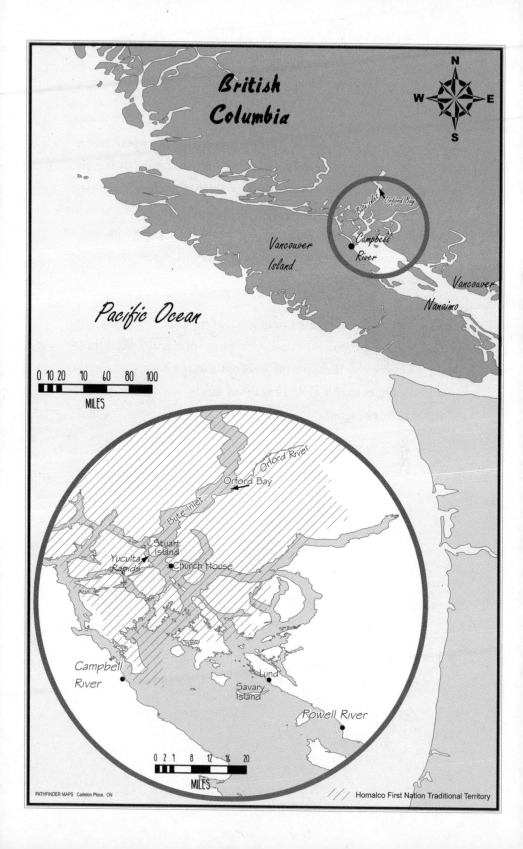

"Up the coast" was my standard answer when anybody asked where I went in the summer, where my father lived nine months of the year, and where I learned to gut fish, shoot a gun, use an axe, and steer a tugboat. It was a catch-all phrase and never elicited any further questions because, for most people, "up the coast" was a vague place somewhere north of Vancouver, with endless forests, a rugged coastline, and not much else.

There was no point in trying to explain that my father's logging camp was situated on the shores of one of the most spectacular fjords in the world. I loved going there for the freedom and the beauty, and sitting around the kitchen table at night with my family, telling stories by the light of a kerosene lamp.

Disclaimer: Life is complex and detailed, and to have told the stories in *Up The Coast* in such a way would have left the reader feeling as if they were listening to someone recount amusing tales about every cat they had owned. Therefore, while most of the events I have written about did take place in Orford Bay, that is not entirely the case. Logging camps moved around a lot, dictated by the government-granted areas they could log. I have also created some characters and presented others as composites of more than one person. Plus, the names of most people in *Up The Coast* have been changed.

Contents

Chapter One

Flying In

Beaver seaplane in Orford Bay. Note the linked chain of logs called a stiff leg, which passengers had to walk along to reach shore.

I CAN SEE THE WATER FAR BELOW FROM THE COCKPIT OF THE bush plane.[1] I'm sitting up front with the pilot. He says I won't get in the way like some of the big sons-of-bitches he flies into camps, and I can understand his point; I'm eight years old. Behind us, the seats are taken up by my mum, my two older sisters, Suzy and Wendy, a drunk logger (who dumped his case of beer into the empty seat next to him so he could enjoy a few inflight beverages), and an Indigenous man who is going home after a stay at the hospital in Campbell River. He still looks sick to me, but maybe he just hates flying, and we are having a bumpy ride today. The pilot said the winds were "blustery" when he was talking into his radio receiver. At least that's what I think he said because we can't hear much over the roar of the engine.

The dashboard is right at my eye level, and there's lots to look at, like all the round dials with arrows that shake like the drunk logger in the back. One of the dials is smashed, and I wonder what it was for, but I guess it's not that important. The pilot looks exactly as he should: khaki shirt and pants, aviator sunglasses, and a handsome face. He smiles but he's like a doctor, doesn't want to get too friendly. Though he did make a joke about gassing up the plane before we took off, something about how he hoped he remembered to refuel. I bet he tells that joke all the time.

---

1 A de Havilland Beaver bush plane, known as the "workhorse of the north."

There's no hold in the plane so everything gets packed inside the cabin. Way at the back in the tail of the plane, there's an outboard motor with a tag on it that reads: "Repaired for Joseph Charlie, Squirrel Cove," and a few life jackets are back there too with some of our suitcases piled on top of them. The biggest suitcases are in the aisle. The last item in the plane was the pilot's fishing rod. He threaded it between the passengers and luggage and hooked it up above the windows on one side. I know he will stop somewhere on his way back home to fish off the Beaver's pontoons. But first he has to drop everybody off, just like a bus driver. Our family will be his last stop because we are going to Orford Bay, way up Bute Inlet where my father lives most of the time. He's a logger.

Out my side window, the forests go on forever and inlets run in every direction, slicing into the coastline and leaving islands scattered along the way. Everything is green: the water, the land, and today, even the sky. Looking down, I see a fishboat with its net out in a big circle. I wonder if it's Uncle Floyd's boat. He fishes when he's not working in our camp. We fly over independent outfits run by loggers who live in their camps year-round, getting by on meagre incomes, government cheques, and canned food. It's easy to spot those camps from the air because there's always lots of broken-down equipment all over the place. Some of these guys drink too much, especially after their wives leave for good. We spot a tug towing a boom of logs and nudge each other, pointing at the logs and smiling because this is the one and only sign of success in this part of the world; logs in the water mean money in the bank.

A few minutes later, I see a camp like ours: two-room houses bought at government auctions for fifty bucks each. Like Dad, the loggers in this camp live here during the logging season, then go home for the winter, either to a seedy hotel on Vancouver's Downtown Eastside or a new bungalow in the suburbs. Dad says it all depends on good luck, hard work, and not being stupid with your money.

The Beaver lands to drop off the drunk logger at a small camp, and he has a hard time getting down the steps of the plane. We all know he's going to be fired on the spot. Nobody wants a drunk logger. I feel sorry for him. Other than the case of beer, he has a small cardboard suitcase and his boots are tied together by the laces and hang around his neck. Next, the Indigenous man is dropped off. I think the whole village was on the dock to greet him. He looked better once he was out of the plane.

The Beaver is lighter now, and I think we are going faster, heading straight up Bute Inlet. I'm excited and press my cheek against the window, trying to see what's up ahead. I know our camp will appear any minute now, but I'm not prepared when the plane banks hard to the right and the undersides of the pontoons are skimming along the cliff face on the north side of Orford Bay. I lean away from the cockpit door, afraid that it will pop open and I'll drop out as the Beaver continues in a sweeping arc round the valley behind camp before levelling off and heading back towards the inlet. Our camp whizzes by underneath the belly of the plane, and the whitecaps come up fast to meet us. The pontoons hit the water hard, *Bang! Bang! Bang!* Then the plane rolls from side to side in the choppy waves. The pilot radios the airport in Campbell River to say we've landed, and he turns the plane around and taxis to the log float out front of camp.

There's our house on the left, then the tool shed. Next is the cook-house, then the bunkhouse, and after that the house where our cousins Ruby and Donna stay when they come for the summer to be with their parents, Aunty Patty and Uncle Floyd. I'm looking for any sign of life but there's nobody around, not even Franky who is usually outside roaring around in his speedboat. He and I are the same age, and I like him but he's usually in trouble because his mum isn't around to smarten him up. His dad is Kurt Wankel, my father's business partner. I can see Uncle Floyd way out on the boom and I notice Aunty Patty has painted a big Thunderbird on the side of their house. She's always doing stuff like that. The Beaver turns again, and the cliffs over by the river come into view, but I can't really see anything, and I suppose the pilot can't either. That's good because it's a secret and we aren't supposed to talk about it. Anyhow, I don't care about that now because the pilot got out and he's tying the Beaver up to the float.

There's Dad! He's walking out our front door to meet the plane, and right on his heels is our dog, Smokey, excited and wagging his tail. Dad shakes hands with the pilot and I hear him say, "How's it goin', Dave? How's the fishin'? Get yourself a cup of coffee in the cookhouse." Then we hear Dad's caulk boots scraping along the pontoon, and he reaches up and pulls open the passenger door and says, "Well, isn't this nice. Here youse all are, eh."

It's 1960 and this is where my story begins—except for the story that comes before it.

Chapter Two

A Normal Childhood

*Bilingual magic tricks, stovetop taxidermy,
swimming while drunk, and other acts of desperation.*

Leaving Home

"I was born in 1921 in North Bay, Ontario. I had a pretty normal childhood."
—John Brandon Willcock

IT WAS MAY 1935, SMACK IN THE MIDDLE OF THE GREAT Depression, when my father left his home in North Bay, Ontario, and boarded a CPR train bound for British Columbia. He was heading out west to find work. John Brandon Willcock was fourteen years old, travelling alone, and it was the first time he had ever left the city of North Bay, let alone been on a train. He was assigned a bench seat, the steerage class of train travel, and for six days and nights he sat on that wooden seat with a box of food on his lap that was so big he couldn't see over the top of it. My grandmother had packed enough food to last a month because she didn't believe the train could cross the vast landscapes of Canada in under a week. My grandfather had run out of ways to make a living in the midst of the Great Depression, and now it was my father's turn to find a way to support his parents and five sisters.

Grandpa had written to his brother, George, who lived on a small island off the coast of British Columbia, inquiring about jobs for my dad, and he heard back from George that loggers made good wages, "even though, as you mentioned in your letter, John is small for his age." George also agreed to "take the boy in for a few days until he gets hired on at a camp."

It wasn't that my grandfather hadn't tried his best to find work. Occasionally, he got night shifts in the CPR rail yards in North Bay, which earned him enough money to keep the wolf from the door, but not the bill collectors. In desperation, he had embarked on a series of wacky money-making schemes.

His first plan was to take his magic show on the road. He was a self-taught magician and believed he had enough tricks up his sleeve to amaze crowds all across the great province of Ontario and maybe even into Québec as well, because, "the show can be translated into real good French," Grandpa declared, "if I just keep saying 'trays magnafeek' and 'voilas.'" But first, he had to literally get the show on the road. The fact he didn't own a vehicle or know how to drive were mere details to my optimistic grandfather.

My father kept a record of some of Grandpa's most memorable escapades in a diary:

"Dad got an old truck on credit. The truck was parked out back of our house and sat there for several weeks until he decided that maybe driving wasn't so hard after all. He told me to go down to the end of the lane and watch for cars. He got the truck out of our yard and pointed away from my end of the lane. Then, by mistake, he slammed the truck into reverse and came hell-bent towards me and I had to jump out of the way as he sailed past me in reverse through the neighbour's fence, across the street, and into a ditch."

Eventually, Grandpa did learn to drive, but he never made any payments on the truck and was in danger of having it repossessed. In December 1933, undeterred, he came up with a new business plan: he would make a killing selling Christmas trees to people who were poorer than he was. A truckload of trees was summarily "liberated" from Crown land and my father was sent out to the tenements in town to sell "Classic Christmas Conifers,"—a label Grandpa was sure justified the price of one dollar each.

"*These tenements were about three storeys high and a lady would say, 'Bring me a tree so I can look at it.' I would drag it up the stairs and she would tell me it wasn't bushy enough, so I would go and get another one. After Christmas, there were quite a few trees left over and I remember when the motor car company came and took the truck away.*"

Despite the setback, Grandpa decided that since he no longer had a truck and he wasn't going to become Eastern Canada's answer to Houdini, he would use his talents to thrill local audiences. He just had to get some rabbits. My father was dispatched to find a couple of small ones, because, as everyone knows, a fat rabbit is hell to pull out of a hat. However, Dad selected the biggest rabbits he could find since the rabbits were going to retire to a stewpot after their acting careers were over. The obese rabbits made for some nerve-wracking moments on stage for Grandpa, but the stews were delicious. Besides, pulling rabbits out of a hat was just Grandpa's warm-up trick. His real crowd-pleaser was cramming his eldest daughter, Margy, into a locked trunk from which she'd vanished. Though, truth be told, she was chubby, and Grandpa had a difficult time getting her in and out of the trunk—similar to his rabbit problem but with no culinary compensation.

"*We got Margy into the trunk which was tough because she was really too big to fit, then we wrapped chains around the trunk and it was locked up with big padlocks. The local chief of police was asked to come up and check the trunk and, after he poked at it a few times, a curtain was pulled across and Dad said, 'Abracadabra.' When the trunk was opened, Margy was gone. This trick was really slick and got people wound up so they were willing to pay an extra ten cents to see Dad's two-headed calf—which gave him the idea for his next business venture: taxidermy.*"

Once Grandpa became a taxidermist, the family home was infused with the aroma of moose heads boiling on the woodstove. Most of his business came from "The Great Moose Club of Greater Northern Ontario." The club members would knock on my grandparents' back door with moose heads in tow, wanting the heads stuffed so they could mount them on their living room walls to impress their friends and make their wives really happy.

The stuffed moose head business naturally flowed into my grandparents' catering business. The Great Moose Club of Greater Northern Ontario often hosted big dinners to celebrate their moose-hunting victories, and they hired my grandparents to cook turkeys for these occasions—which may seem counterintuitive, but if you've ever eaten a moose roast, you will appreciate turkey.

"Mum and Dad would stay up all night cooking turkeys. I don't know how they did it because they only had one stove, though we ate well because some of those turkeys went to the club missing a leg, which nobody noticed because those guys drank a lot."

In the spring of 1934, Grandpa added one more source of income to the family coffers. He started up an in-house laundry service where all the sheets from a nearby hotel were washed and ironed by the Willcock family. My grandmother just added a couple of copper boilers to the top of the woodstove and they were in business.

"The laundry was working out just fine until we started getting complaints from the hotel. The guests said the sheets smelled like moose, so we lost that business, too."

Not long after the "it smells like there's a moose in my bed" incident, my grandfather came up with the idea of sending my father out west. It wasn't going to cost him a dime because his semi-not-very-often-at-all job with the CPR gave employees free tickets—but as everyone knows, "free travel" is usually not all that comfy.

"Once the train got underway, I started to get excited. I rented a pillow for the trip and it cost 25 cents and I slept on the bench seat. At night, the conductor would come around and want to see my pass, so I didn't sleep so good. Also, my box of food took up a seat and the conductor told me I had to move it since I only had one free seat, not two. After that, when I saw him coming, I'd put the box on my lap, but I couldn't see over the top of it. The other problem was my suit. My mother got it for me from one of her relatives on the reserve and she altered the jacket but didn't have time to alter the pants, so every time I got up to walk around, I had to hold on to my pants so they wouldn't fall down.

"Everything was going real good until we pulled into Winnipeg where I had to change trains. I put my food box and suitcase on top of a locker and walked into town. There was a lot to see and I got carried away and forgot about the time. When I got back to the station, the train was gone. A CPR employee saw me wandering around and I told him what had happened. He said I could come home with him and get the train the next day. He had a nice wife and children so I stayed with them and caught the train in the morning."

By the time the train pulled into Vancouver, Dad's box of food was still brimming with jars of pickled beets, fruitcake, and cheese sandwiches. He somehow made his way to the Union Steamship dock on Carrall Street carrying the box while keeping a firm grip on his pants, and when he finally boarded the steamship *Chelohsin* for the trip up the coast, he couldn't believe his luck. Free meals were served in the dining room—goodbye cheese sandwiches, hello roast beef dinners!

"On board, the chief steward rang a gong and everyone trooped into the dining room. The tables were all nicely set with white linen tablecloths and gleaming silverware, but I had never eaten with more than a knife and fork so the waiter told me which utensils to use every time he put something new on my plate."

When the ship docked at Stuart Island, Uncle George was there to meet Dad.

"My uncle looked me over, and I don't think he approved of what he saw because he didn't say anything. He had been an officer in the British Army during WWI and I guess he expected that I would be more like a soldier and less like a runt."

Stuart Island General Store. My parents' future house is on the left.

STUART ISLAND

THE HORRORS OF TRENCH WARFARE HAD LEFT UNCLE GEORGE longing for a quiet life in a remote corner of the empire, so he packed up his life in England and headed west, not stopping until he reached the tiny community of Stuart Island, situated on the far left side of his map of Canada. Peace at last.

He just had to find a way to make a living. He didn't want to log. It reminded him too much of the war, with all the noise and equipment mired in mud, and fishing was too damned wet and cold. Then he found the perfect opportunity. It was right under his nose. Stuart Island had a general store that wasn't well stocked and was only open for business when the owners felt like it or were sober—and it was for sale.

It took him less than a year to revive the failing business. The store got regular hours and fully stocked shelves with everything from cream soda to Christmas decorations from Japan, plus all the basics loggers required, like work gloves, suspenders, and long underwear with buttons on the front and back—a convenience that allowed men the luxury of not changing their long johns for months at a time.

Uncle George ran the store with military precision and an unwavering dedication to duty, and he expected nothing less from his employees, including my father.

"Uncle George put me to work right away. His years in the army had left him with the idea that young men should be kept busy, and he also knew how to give orders. One of my jobs was to move freight from the dock to the store. Every ten days freight was delivered by steamship from Vancouver and it took about two hours to unload everything onto the dock, so there was a big pile of it.

"My first Boat Day on the island, my uncle showed me where the wheelbarrow was and told me to bring the freight up from the dock. I started piling boxes and crates into the wheelbarrow, not realizing that I was the only guy moving freight. The walk up to the store went along the dock for about one hundred feet then up a ramp fifty feet long. At low tide, this ramp was at a seventy-five-degree slope and for all the months I was at Stuart Island the freight boat always arrived at low tide. I used to think the captain waited for low tide until he docked. Loggers from the camps in the area came to Stuart Island on Boat Day for their supplies including big piles of boom chains. The weight of the chains tilted the dock so far over that it became submerged in about a foot of water and that made the trips with the wheelbarrow a little tougher.

"In between freight deliveries, my uncle thought up all kinds of things for me to do. He had me build miles of trails all over the island; they didn't go anyplace but the job kept me occupied. Another job was to chop wood for his cookstove and stack it neatly according to his precise instructions. I chopped enough wood to last for about ten years. For all this work, I was paid ten dollars a month and it didn't take me long to figure out I was going in the hole twenty dollars a month after I paid Uncle George for room and board. I couldn't wait to get a job in a logging camp.

"My big break was sort of forced on me. One day, I was bringing the freight up from the dock and I found a case of 'Stomach Bitters' with two broken bottles inside. My uncle used to sell the bitters in the store.

The stuff was supposed to help upset stomachs but had a very high alcohol content and only cost $1.20 for a twenty-six-ounce bottle. It was the cheapest hooch on the coast. I had always wanted to try the stuff so I got an empty pop bottle and poured the remains of the two broken bottles into it. After I finished work that day, I started to drink and I got really drunk and became worried because I had to sober up before sitting down for dinner with my uncle.

"Up behind the store there was a dam, which held our water supply. I figured if I went there and stuck my head in the water, it would sober me up. Well, my uncle found me in the reservoir with all my clothes on spluttering around trying to figure out how to get out. It's a miracle I didn't drown. The next day I was told to pack my things which was fine by me.

"Luckily, it was Boat Day the following day and I went down to the dock and asked a few of the logging operators who had come to pick up supplies if they needed any help. Gus Swanberg, an old Swede, had a logging camp about forty miles up Bute Inlet and he said he needed someone to help out in the cookhouse. When I got my suitcase out of the store and was heading down to Gus's boat, I caught a glimpse of my uncle standing in the entrance of the store. He looked relieved to be getting rid of me. I had never lived up to his expectations, and he had always reminded me of that in case I had any ideas to the contrary. But his attitude was a great motivator, and as the camp boat pulled away from the dock, I was more determined than ever to become successful."

Chapter Three
Fired or Dead

Cautionary tales about riding the rails, pet cougars, and cutting trees down from the inside out.

My fourteen-year-old father at his first logging camp.

GREASY ERIKSON

IN HIS DIARY, MY FATHER DESCRIBED HIS JOB AS A FLUNKY IN Swanberg's cookhouse:

"*The run from Stuart Island to Swanberg's camp took six hours. I sat on the deck of the tug and I couldn't take my eyes off the towering peaks on either side of the inlet. Even in the middle of the summer they were snow-capped and I wondered how men could log on these steep mountainsides.*

"*We arrived in camp just before supper and Gus told me to report to the cook. I was excited to finally have a job in a logging camp even if it was just in the cookhouse. I thought I could cool my heels, help out the cook a few times a day and wait for a chance to get a job up the hill.*[2]

"*The cook's name was Erikson and he was a fat, old Swede who the crew called 'Greasy Erikson' because every morsel of food that came out of his kitchen had a thick layer of grease congealing on top of it.*

"*I had a small room off the dining room just big enough for a bed and a small table. I had to get up at 5:00 am to get the fire going in the cookstove and put the water on to boil, then wake the cook. After that, I had to go into the bunkhouse and washhouse and light the woodstoves in there all the while trying to be as quiet as I could because you don't want to wake loggers before they have to get up.*

---

2 *Up the hill* was an expression loggers used when referring to any mountainous logging operation, no matter how precipitous.

"*The tables in the cookhouse were always set the night before so my main job at breakfast was to serve the food. The dining room was separate from the kitchen so I was kept busy running back and forth. Nobody talked much in the morning; the loggers would push their plates towards me if they wanted more food, and simply lift their mugs up for coffee refills. Once they were done, they'd just get up and walk out.*

"*After breakfast, when I had cleaned up the kitchen and washed the dishes, I would sweep the bunkhouse and make the beds. Some of the old-timers would make their own beds which helped me out a lot. Next, I had to fill all the coal oil lamps because this was the only source of light in the camp. There were about thirty lamps in total. At lunchtime, there was just the cook, the boom man[3] and me so there wasn't too much for me to do in the kitchen, which gave me time to cut firewood. The camp was all on floats and I cut the logs into lengths in the water with a six-foot dragsaw,[4] then pulled the cut pieces up on the float with a hand winch and stacked them into piles to dry. This job took me to dinnertime, and I finished up the dishes around 8:00 pm and fell into bed with my clothes on and didn't move until the next morning at 5:00 when it all started over again.*

"*One day, Erikson told me to go out to a fishboat that was tied up to the log boom and get two salmon the fisherman had for us. I got the fish, carrying one in each hand by the gills, and as I was walking back to camp along the boomsticks,[5] I slipped and fell in the water. I tried to swim with a twenty-pound salmon in each hand but I kept going under. After thrashing around for some time, I let go of one fish but that was still no good. I was getting tired because I had my coat and boots on and I wasn't the best swimmer in the world so I let the other salmon go, too. The beach looked a long way off and when I got to shallow water where*

---

3 A *boom man* is a logger who works on logs that have been dumped into the ocean for sorting.
4 *Dragsaws* were the first mechanized saws used in the logging industry and the predecessor of the chainsaw. They had a six-foot blade, weighed about 400 pounds, and were powered by a steam winch.
5 *Boomsticks* are floating logs chained together to form a boom or enclosure around loose logs.

I could touch my feet on the bottom, I just stood in the freezing water for a few minutes to catch my breath. When I showed up at the cookhouse dripping wet, the cook didn't give a damn that I had nearly drowned, he just screamed 'What the hell am I gonna cook for dinner, you imbecile!' The loggers didn't have any sympathy for me either because they had Spam for dinner that night.

"Greasy Erickson also drank a lot and he made his own hooch. Every Saturday, Gus Swanberg would go to Stuart Island for the mail and freight, and as soon as his boat was out of sight, the cook got his still working on a new batch of hooch. A big pot of fermented fruit was placed on the stove with a bowl on top of it, and over that was a wash basin of cool water, then the whole thing was sealed with tea towels. My job was to keep changing the water in the basin when it got warm. It must have been strong stuff because the cook got very drunk, which was okay by me because this was the only time he was halfway pleasant, but in the morning when he was hungover, my life became a living hell.

"His terrible cooking eventually became inedible. Each morning I would take plates of raw hotcakes to the men, who sent me back to the kitchen with them, and Erikson would send me right back out with them again screaming, 'Those bastards don't know good food!' For all of this I was paid fifty dollars a month, but I was happy to be in a logging camp and knew my big break would come."

Whistle Punk

"SWANBERG'S CAMP HAD A LONG SKYLINE CONNECTED TO A *towering spar tree.[6] The steam donkey[7] would pull the logs into the spar tree, then they would be sent one at a time screaming through the air down the skyline to crash into the water with a huge splash. From the cookhouse, I could hear the donkey working and the whistle blowing up the hill, and I couldn't wait to go to work up there. Then one day, Gus told me that his nephew was coming up to camp to work in the cookhouse and I was going to be sent up the hill to work as a whistle punk.[8]*

"I was finally going to be a logger and I was the happiest guy in the world! I had prepared for this opportunity. Under my bed I had tucked away an old pair of caulk boots my uncle had given me. They were too big but I didn't care. Besides, every morning around five o'clock I'd watch*

---

6   A *spar tree* was a tall tree stripped of its branches and rigged with cables for hauling logs.

7   *Steam donkeys* were steam-powered winches that hauled logs on cables attached to the spar tree.

8   *Whistle punks* were usually young guys without much logging experience. From high on a mountainside, they positioned themselves to have a bird's-eye view of the logging operation, and their job was to blow a combination of long or short blasts on a whistle to let the "donkey" or steam winch operator know when to haul on the cables to drag logs across the mountainside. The whistle punk had to focus intently to ensure cables did not get snagged on stumps or rocks because taut cables could snap and kill loggers on the ground.

the steam engineer leave camp and begin the hour long walk up the hill in order to get the steam up in the donkey in time for the rest of the crew to begin work a few hours later. This old Swede had a wooden leg and I don't know how he managed that climb every day, but I knew I would have it easier up the hill than he did.

"Blowing whistles on the steam donkey was a good job for a fifteen-year-old, but I wanted to get up in the world so I brought a piece of cable back to the bunkhouse because I wanted to learn how to splice (mend) *cable. Most of the loggers were too tired at night to show me how to do it, but one old-timer taught me, and I learned how to put in an eye splice that would hold a broken cable together under great pressure. I figured that you had to catch on fast when you were working in the woods or you would end up fired or dead."*

FER CHRISSAKES! DUCK!

WHEN SWANBERG'S CAMP SHUT DOWN FOR THE SEASON, DAD took a Union Steamship to Vancouver and moved into a cheap hotel on the Downtown Eastside. Every morning, he showed up at the "Loggers Employment Office" looking for work.

"I walked from my hotel over to Howe Street where the office was and got in line with about thirty other guys and waited for the doors to open. When I got up to the front desk, the clerk would take one look at me and snarl, 'No work.' I had been staying at the Niagara Hotel for about three weeks and I was slowly going broke. Then, another logger told me that I just looked too young and if I got in line late in the day the clerk was so tired he didn't even look up at who he was giving jobs to. This is how I got a job in Frederick Arm at a camp called York Logging, a few hours by boat from Stuart Island.

"It was around Christmas when I started working there, and I figured out pretty quick it wasn't a good camp when I walked into the bunkhouse and there were cans hanging all over the ceiling to catch the leaks. You had to remember to empty them or the beds got wet. It was also very cold and I slept under about ten blankets and never took my long underwear off, and I was still cold. The outhouse was just a big long pole across a pit and it would hold four guys at one time. Not very private, but it never broke down.

"We were working in about two feet of snow and sometimes the chainsaws got too wet so the fallers used old crosscut saws instead. I was blowing whistles at this camp, and one day the fallers called me over to an old growth cedar they were cutting down with a crosscut saw. They had the undercut in the tree and could see that it was hollow inside and they needed a small guy to climb into the half-cut tree and cut from the inside out. I climbed inside the tree and they fed me one end of the saw and another logger outside the tree had the other end. Together we sawed and sawed and I was told that when it started to come down to get the hell out of the tree, but all of a sudden we heard a big crack and the tree started to go over. My boss yelled, 'Fer Chrissakes! Duck!' and he and the other guys ran like hell and I was left inside the tree. I closed my eyes and felt it shaking and tearing apart and when it landed the ground all around shook like an earthquake. My boss and the other guys came running up to the trunk of the tree and saw me hunched over inside the stump. I think they were surprised I was still alive but nobody said anything."

Off the Rails

"ANOTHER CAMP I WORKED FOR WAS CALLED FLETCHER LOGG-
ing, a railway camp way up in Phillips Arm that employed about 150
men and put about twenty-five cars of logs into the water every day. I
was sixteen when I worked there and I was happy that I was getting
experience in a different kind of logging. The camp was run by Mrs.
Fletcher. I had never worked in a camp run by a woman, but she was a
pretty good boss.

"In the morning, the 'locie'[9] blew the train whistle to wake everyone
up. We would go into the old log cookhouse, and there was a big lunch
table with piles of sandwiches and cookies, and we'd load up our lunch
buckets, adding a thermos of coffee, and then we went into the dining hall
and had breakfast. Nobody talked unless they had a complaint about the
food and even then the guys just said a few words like 'no good' or 'burnt'
and shoved their plates aside. I never said a word because I was always
the youngest on the crew.

"After breakfast, we went out to the train and headed for work about
eight miles back in the valley. The fallers had their own car on the train
because they were the elite guys and got paid more than the other loggers. I watched them every morning with their long falling and bucking
saws they had filed the night before. Nobody touched their saws because
they were like jagged razors. They were independent contractors and just

---

9   A *locie* is a locomotive operator.

moved from camp to camp falling trees and making money, but it wasn't a job I wanted because a lot of those guys got killed.

"One afternoon, the train went off the tracks and the crew had to walk back to camp. Four of us young guys found an old handcar beside the tracks and we lifted it onto the tracks, piled in, and headed back to camp. It was all downhill and all we had for brakes was a pole rubbing against the wheel. The pole wore out in about five minutes, and we were going to beat hell, probably around 60 mph, when we bailed out. It's a wonder none of us were killed."

HERE, KITTY, KITTY

"ACROSS THE INLET FROM FLETCHER'S WAS A HAND LOGGER *named August Schnarr who had three daughters. His wife had died and he raised the girls by himself. The girls, named Pansy, Pearl, and Marion, were around my age, and they had been helping their dad hand log for years. When August felled a tree into the water, the girls would take a boat, hook onto the log, tow it into camp, and put it in their boom.*

"The loggers in camp kept encouraging me to pay a visit to the girls, so at the first opportunity I hopped in a rowboat and rowed over to their camp. I suppose the guys thought this was pretty funny because I didn't know the girls kept two good size cougars as pets. About a year earlier, August had been out in the bush hunting and ran into the mother cougar near her den. He was able to shoot her before she attacked and he brought her cubs back to camp in his backpack. The cubs were about the size of regular house cats then and they took to the girls immediately.

"As I walked into their camp, I could see two cougars chained up to a tree. They were almost full grown and I could feel them watching me. I was terrified. As I got closer, they started pulling on their chains. The girls were nowhere to be seen; it was just me and the cougars and they were hissing and showing their teeth. I didn't want to turn my back on them so I just stood still until the girls finally showed up. They told me the only reason the cougars were chained was because they got defensive when strangers came around; otherwise they roamed free since the girls

couldn't provide a steady supply of raw meat for them. This didn't make me feel too relaxed.

"When I got up to leave, I had to turn my back to the cougars and I could hear them pulling on their chains and hissing, but I didn't run because I didn't want that getting back to the loggers in camp."[10]

10 See: Judith Williams, *Raincoast Chronicles #24, Cougar Companions, Bute Inlet Country and the Legendary Schnarrs* (Madeira Park, B.C.: Harbour Publishing Co. Ltd., 2019).

Marion Schnarr with one of her pet cougars.

Chapter Four

That's the Navy for You

*The war years: my mother has the time of her life, and my father joins
the navy and narrowly escapes dying of stupidity.*

Sailors on leave, strolling along Granville Street in Vancouver.
My father is on the right.

Rosie the Riveter

IN 1944, MY MOTHER, JOAN O'CONNELL, WAS EIGHTEEN YEARS old and had everything a teenager could want: money in her pocket, a string of admirers, and no parents around to tell her what to do. Along with two of her sisters, Mildred and Hilda, she had moved to Vancouver from the family farm in Fort Langley, rented a house on Laurel Street, and was having a hell of a good time.

She had wasted no time getting herself a "Rosie the Riveter" job at the Boeing Aircraft plant located in Richmond, a few miles from Vancouver. This was one of the best wartime jobs for women, paying a generous wage of one dollar per hour. At its peak of production, Boeing employed a workforce of around seven thousand men and women who worked round the clock manufacturing aircraft for the war effort, including the bomb bays for the Boeing Superfortress (B-29) bombers and Catalina aircraft for offshore patrols. Mum became the first female "journeyman riveter" in the plant and documented her days on and off the job in letters to her sister Doreen who had joined the Wrens[11] and was stationed in Scotland.

In response to overwhelming Japanese victories in the Pacific, the pace of work at Boeing was flat out. In one letter, Mum complained, *"It was so hot in our shop today and we're so busy because we're far behind and are trying to catch up."* The number of rivets each woman did per

---

11 The *Wrens* were the Women's Royal Canadian Naval Service.

shift was carefully tallied, and Mum reported to Doreen that, *"There was a record set at work the other night on the late shift. A team did 5,181 rivets. The foreman told Bob, our lead hand, about it, but Bob set him back on his heels when he said Elinor and Wilda were doing 6,750 in their shift."* The frantic pace of work was probably the cause of an accident Mum had, *"drilling through one of my fingers the other day, and it's proper swollen and sore and the nail is crushed off."*

However, she enjoyed spending her hard-earned money and sent Doreen a list of the luxuries she bought, including vinyl records of the latest hits, such as "I'm Beginning to See the Light," "Let's Take the Long Way Home," and "Cocktails for Two," which, my mother wrote, *"didn't impress Mildred and Hilda much at first but when it really started they practically jumped off the chesterfield."* Also, for the first time in her life, Mum spent money on new clothes, admitting in one of her letters, *"I did quite a bit of shopping and bought a new aqua-blue suit and an alligator purse that's got a place for gloves, and cost $8.00, and a new spring hat that is gold with a brown band and has a veil. It's very smart and sits on the front of my head. I spent all my money and I've got $1.79 to last me for two weeks."* She included a drawing of the hat along with her new hairdo, which she described as *"rolled under at the front and really pretty classy."*

With new clothes and a new hairstyle, she was ready for an exciting social life and didn't have long to wait. She went out jitterbugging at the Commodore Ballroom on Granville Street, hiking up Hollyburn Mountain, suntanning on the beaches of West Vancouver, and dating lots of young enlisted men who were either waiting to be shipped off or were returning home on leave. One of her suitors, George, often took her to see the wartime movies Hollywood was churning out, like *Casablanca*, while Mum wrote to Doreen about another young man called Jimmy who *"brought me a lovely corsage of red roses. It was really beautiful. Then we went out to dinner at Malcolm's Steakhouse and had some champagne."* Her next letter describes a party at the Laurel Street house: *"Last night Lloyd, Kenny, and Rocky came over, and Stan came up after. The night before last George and Al, and Andy, and Gordon and Stan were here and we danced all night in our stocking feet. People will wonder if we are running a bootleg joint, but of course it is just us popular girls."* But Mum didn't stop there. At work she was also flirting, and hurriedly ended a letter to Doreen with the hopeful words, *"I've got my eye on the crane operator; he waves every time I go by. Well, time to get my coveralls on."*

But tragedy was bound to strike; it was wartime after all. My mother's special boyfriend, Frank, who was with the First Canadian Army in Holland, wrote to her in February 1944 saying he thought he'd be home for Christmas. He also let her know he and his fellow soldiers had been fighting in towns and villages flooded with seawater after the Dutch had broken dykes in an attempt to handicap the Germans who weren't giving up easily. Then, his letters stopped coming and my mother thought he was on his way home, but after a month she got the last letter she had written to him returned with "Deceased" stamped all over it and a note attached stating, "The Postmaster General deeply regrets the circumstances under which this letter is returned." In an anguished note to Doreen, my mother wrote, *"I wish they had destroyed it"* (the letter). *"I still can't believe he's dead but I guess there are millions of people who feel this way. He asked me to marry him—the returned letter was my answer so he never knew how I felt."*

The only other record of Frank appeared in a letter to Doreen written about a year before his death. He often visited my mother and her sisters in the evenings, and as they sat around talking and drinking tea, he would mend Mum's socks. She wrote, *"He sure is a nice fellow. He did a lovely job on my socks—a lot better than I could have done myself."*

On V.E. Day, May 8, 1945, Mum marked the Allied victory in Europe by joining the celebrations in downtown Vancouver, describing the joy and chaos in one of her letters to Doreen: *"Last night, is a thing I'll never forget in all my life! Everyone had flags, hats, horns, and whistles, and they were making as much noise as they possibly could. There was a parade of about 300 people going down Seymour St. led by several airmen beating on pots and pans they had 'borrowed' from a nearby restaurant. Over on Granville Street there were decorated cars all with about twenty people hanging on the outside, mostly sailors (that's the Navy for you), and people marched down the street while streamers of toilet paper hung from the windows and over all the streetcar wires. Confetti also rained down and carpeted the street. The best thing was a long conga line led by a blonde and her sailor. They were both wearing hats they had got 'on loan' from a store nearby and the tags were hanging down their backs. There was also a piper in his kilt on top of a car playing his heart out, but he couldn't play over the clamour of a car that came down Granville Street with a train bell fixed up on the front of it. Police tried to conduct traffic but just gave up."*

In contrast, my father's V.E. Day celebrations were somewhat less exciting. He was with a few close friends locked up in Powell River's only jail cell. The young men had spent the previous four years together in the navy riding the big rollers off Vancouver Island and Haida Gwaii, doing their damnedest to avoid the Japanese submarines lurking beneath the waves. Dad had joined the navy at seventeen (lying about his age) when a recruiting boat docked at Stuart Island looking for men who knew the coast and how to operate a boat in high seas without puking their guts out. But now, that's exactly what my father and his friends were doing: puking their guts out on the floor of a jail cell. The sailors had been arrested for being "inebriated and overly exuberant," which was the official way of stating they had been acting like idiots, (something my father excelled at, having been arrested a year earlier in Prince Rupert for fighting—other sailors, not the enemy). Later, the arresting officer told the young men, "You might have killed yourselves, and I didn't want to have to tell your mothers their sons died of stupidity on the last day of the war."

John and Joan, 1946

How Would Youse Like to Dance?

MY PARENTS MET ON A SATURDAY NIGHT AT THE COMMODORE Ballroom on Granville Street. It was December 1945; the war was over, and it was time to have some fun and find romance. The ballroom had a reputation for sparking young love, which probably had something to do with its sprung dance floor. It had a real bounce to it, encouraging dancers to bust their best moves. But bouncy floor or not, the Commodore was the place to be on a Saturday night. Drinks were cheap, and the band played until the ungodly hour of 1:00 am.

My father showed up at the Commodore with a few of his navy buddies. They were terrified. The young sailors had enjoyed little, if any, contact with women during the war years and now everything they thought they knew about "girls" was all wrong. The women at the Commodore were drinking, smoking, laughing out loud, and even dancing with each other! Women had changed. They were taking charge, not standing on the sidelines of life waiting for an invitation to join in.

Mum and her sisters were right in the thick of things that night. Their hair was rolled to perfection, short skirts swaying to the music, and they knew their way around a dance floor. The war years had been good to them, and they were continuing to enjoy big city life in Vancouver. Not bad for a bunch of farm girls.

Dad was still wearing his navy uniform, the only respectable clothes he had, and he was short and shy and didn't know a jitterbug from a humbug. I imagine him standing off in a corner trying to suck up enough courage from the bottom of a glass to ask my mother to dance. The thought is toe-curling and heartbreaking at the same time, but eventually he pulled himself together and took the long walk across the dance floor to where she stood snapping her fingers to the music. "How would youse like to dance?" he croaked, and she took one look at the terror-stricken sailor standing in front of her and said, "That would be nice," and it was.

They were married a year later and moved up the coast.

Chapter Five

Belly Up

*Suspiciously large babies, the logic of wearing six pairs of underpants,
and a throne for a princess.*

Family Business

BACK ON THE COAST, DAD PARTNERED WITH KURT WANKEL, A friend he had logged with before the war. They formed a company called Willcock & Wankel Logging Ltd., a name with little cachet but representative of two enthusiastic young men with big plans. Their first piece of business was to show up early one November morning in 1947 at the Marine Building in Vancouver. They were there for a timber auction that was about to take place in the offices of the Ministry of Forests—the government agency that controlled the logging industry in British Columbia (they thought so, anyhow). My father and Kurt believed this day would mark the beginning of their lucrative careers in the woods. They had bought shirts and ties for the occasion and borrowed suits from family members who were approximately their size, and they entered the building feeling confident.

Once a logging company was issued a government timber licence, its operators had the go-ahead to clear-cut everything within the boundaries of a specific area called a timber lot (and maybe a few hundred yards beyond the perimeter, if nobody in the ministry was paying attention). Getting a good or bad licence determined whether you were taking the wife and kids to Hawaii for Christmas or visiting a stony-faced banker in December to ask for a loan until you sold some logs the following spring.

Months before the timber auction, Dad and Kurt had chartered a bush plane to fly over the licence areas they were thinking about bidding on. This was called timber cruising, and loggers had to take into consideration not only the quality of timber in each lot but also how many miles of road had to be built to get to it, where the nearest deepwater log dump could be constructed, and if there was a good foreshore for the camp itself. The licence areas my father and Kurt had cruised looked good in all respects, and they were sure they could make money on the timber if the bidding went well. But they forgot to factor in their lying, cheating, stab-you-in-the-back family members.

Enter my uncles Ron and Harold Stearman. They swindled every logger they did business with—but came by it honestly. They had grown up during the Depression and were both working in the woods by the time they were ten years old. This was the era when trees were felled with hand-held crosscut saws and horses did the hauling. The work was just the right combination of danger and back-breaking work to make the brothers into real sons of bitches by the time they reached manhood and got their own logging shows.[12]

Uncle Harold married Aunty Margy, Dad's oldest sister. They met in 1937, shortly after she arrived on Stuart Island to work in Uncle George's general store. She sold made-in-Japan souvenir totem poles to American tourists and essentials to loggers and fishermen including boots, suspenders, flannel shirts, and wall calendars with illustrations of women in negligees working on cars and painting houses (because that's what women liked doing back then). Aunty Margy said she didn't even have to look up from her *Silver Screen* magazine to know who was standing at the counter waiting to pay because she could tell by their smell. American yachtsmen smelled like talcum powder, loggers smelled like diesel and sweat, and fishermen, no surprise, had a distinct fishy aroma. But for some reason, the day Uncle Harold sauntered into the store she looked up and never took her eyes off him. She said he reminded her of James Dean, but about six inches shorter and maybe forty pounds heavier. They were married a few months later and went

---

12 Loggers referred to their logging operations or businesses as *logging shows*.

to live in Uncle Harold's camp in Knight Inlet.

Uncle Harold was charming around friends and family at weddings and funerals, but was a monster to do business with. Get him at a boardroom table, and he didn't give a damn if he was signing off on a deal that would impoverish a family member. But he was great with all the kids in the family, never failing to slip us nickels and dimes, and was more than happy to show us his left hand that was missing two fingers due to an unfortunate miscalculation with an axe.

I'm not exactly sure how Uncle Ron was related to our family, but it was through some kind of marriage, divorce, remarriage situation. His second marriage was to Aunty Lorna who once told me she regretted going to university because there weren't many eligible bachelors around by the time she graduated, and that's how she ended up with Uncle Ron. They bought a big house in North Vancouver, had three kids, and Aunty Lorna spent her time crocheting toilet roll covers resembling weird pink poodles, while waiting for frozen dinners to heat up in her wall oven.

When he was home, Uncle Ron sat in the darkened living room in front of a flickering TV so drunk he didn't move all day. Nobody talked to him. Aunty Lorna emptied his ashtray every once in a while, and brought him meals he never touched. Occasionally, he went "away," which meant he was off on a bender, holed up in a motel room. But every year, when November rolled around, he sobered up and got together with Uncle Harold to plot how they were going to monopolize the best stands of timber on the coast for the coming logging season. Then it was time to show up at the Marine Building and bid on some timber.

At first, the timber auction of November 1947 appeared to be much like all the others. Loggers assembled on the sidewalk in front of the Marine Building's ornate brass doors, clean-shaven, hair Brylcreemed, some wearing the suits they had got married in that were now tight around the arms and across the chest from years of working in the woods. They entered the building and took the elevator to the fifth floor where they walked right past the ministry offices and into the men's washroom at the end of the hall. This was where they settled up with each other before officially presenting their bids to the ministry.

Surrounded by urinals and cracked sinks, the men silently negotiated by writing dollar amounts on the inside flaps of their cigarette packages, then handing them back and forth until there were handshakes of agreement all round. Once the bids were fixed and each man understood what timber licence he would get and what he was going to pay for it, they piled out of the washroom, stinking of sweat and cigarette smoke, to convene in the ministry's boardroom where they sat nervously checking and rechecking the figures scribbled on the inside of their cigarette packs. But soon the bidding would be over and everyone would go out for a steak sandwich and a few beers. At least, that's usually what happened. This time, however, the boardroom door opened and Uncle Ron and Uncle Harold walked in, all smiles and apologies for being late.

They didn't waste any time slapping their bids on the table, sending the bidding process into a free fall as loggers scrambled to increase bids they couldn't afford, while others were left with lousy timber licences, dooming them to a year of meagre profits. Dad and Kurt got nothing, and later, out on the street where they confronted the traitors, Uncle Harold shrugged off their accusations saying, "That's business, boys." Then he and Uncle Ron turned and sauntered up Burrard Street to find a bar and celebrate what was shaping up to be another great year in the woods.

The brothers spent years tearing up the forests along the coast, banking more money than they knew what to do with, other than dig up their backyards for swimming pools they never used and buy new Cadillacs each year that they drove to Reno for the slot machines and free drinks. In retirement, Uncle Harold spent days in his vegetable garden, not interested in much besides the size of his tomatoes and the yield of the raspberry patch—as if he had forgotten what a ruthless son of a bitch he had been. Uncle Ron died in front of the TV, though nobody knew the exact time because he'd been sitting there all day.

A Basket from Moses

I HAVE THE INDIGENOUS CEDAR BASKETS MY MOTHER BOUGHT or was given during the years our family lived up the coast. Inside each one she left a note stating its provenance and date. One note simply reads, "Given to me at Stuart Island, 1952," while another states, "Paid $5.00 for this basket. Mary Charlie made it in 1948." I marvel at my young mother's appreciation for an art form that, at the time, was mostly unrecognized and certainly undervalued outside Indigenous communities.

One basket is large, about two feet in diameter, and equally deep, with a flat lid. A smaller one served as Mum's sewing basket for sixty years. Then there's the baby basket, long and narrow, just the right size for an infant to fit in nice and snug. This one was given to my parents in 1949 by their friend and frequent dinner guest, Moses Charlie, following the birth of my eldest sister, Suzy. At the time, my parents were living at Church House, an Indigenous settlement at the mouth of Bute Inlet, and the basket brought peace to their home in a way they could never have ever imagined.

After Dad and Uncle Kurt had lost their shirts at the timber auction, my parents were desperate for a place to live. At Church House, they were welcomed like family. Never mind that they were not Indigenous people, Dad had worked alongside many of the Church House men in camps when they were all around fourteen years old, scared and lonely for home. Their friendships ran deep.

Every morning, my father rowed to work, and Mum stayed home and got an accelerated education in community living. Suzy was not a good sleeper, but she was a champion crier, which the ladies on the reserve frequently pointed out to Mum in case she hadn't noticed. They'd stick their heads in the kitchen door and say, "Joan, your baby's crying," or sometimes they'd shout through an open window: "Joan, Suzy's awake." Mum said she was too embarrassed to ask for help and was left to wonder why she had got a baby who was an insomniac.

And then there was their neighbour, Moses, who dropped in every night just as Mum and Dad were sitting down to eat. He'd open the back door, walk in, sit down on the sofa, and say, "That smells real good." What could my parents do? They invited him for dinner.

Moses, like my parents, was in his early twenties and had a wife and kids, so Mum and Dad couldn't figure out why he wanted to have dinner at their house every night, but they were too polite to ask. After a few weeks, there were long pauses between the riveting conversation topics about how good or bad the fishing was and how hard it was going to blow up the inlet the next day. Dinnertime became a strain, the silence broken only by Suzy's vocal warm-ups for the long night ahead.

Then one day Moses stopped coming for dinner. After a week had gone by and he hadn't returned, Mum went to his house and asked him if there was a problem. Was it her cooking? Had she and Dad offended him in some way, or was Suzy driving him crazy? Moses reassured her he had not been insulted and her dinners were pretty good except sometimes she overcooked the vegetables. He went on to explain that the month before he'd had a fight with his wife, Annie, and she threw him out. He'd moved in with his sister, but she was a bad cook, so he thought he'd give my mother's cooking a try. Then his wife had taken him back, so he wouldn't be coming for dinner anymore and he was sorry about that. As Mum turned to go, Moses asked her to wait a minute and he went into the house and came back with a baby basket. He said he and Annie, who had made the basket for their kids, thought it might help Suzy sleep.

He told Mum to swaddle Suzy in a blanket, making sure to tuck her arms in, place her in the basket, and lace her in, using the loops running along the sides of the basket, the same way you lace shoes. After that, all Mum and Dad had to do was hang the basket on the wall above their bed at night and if Suzy began to fuss, they could reach up and give the basket a nudge and it would rock back and forth on the wall like a metronome. "It works real good," Moses said. "Our kids liked it." Mum had her doubts but she and Dad were willing to give it a try, and before long Suzy was sleeping through the night. A year later, when they moved to Stuart Island, they made sure to take the basket with them in case the next baby that came along was also an insomniac.

ROUND AND ROUND

SHORTLY AFTER THEY ARRIVED ON STUART ISLAND, MY SISTER, Wendy, was born, and my parents decided to spend some of their hard-earned money on a permanent family home now that they were a family of four. In a letter to Doreen, my mother wrote, "The house cost thirty dollars and is a little bigger than our last place. It's sitting on pylons, right on the beach in Big Bay next to the general store and when the tide is out, the floor sags, but at high tide it's quite even. John and Kurt finally got a timber licence of their own in Ramsay Arm, about ten miles from here, and John is going to winch the house onto a log float and tow it behind our tug to the new campsite in Fanny Bay. I think it will be an easy move as the girls and I can stay in the house and just go along for the ride." What my mother did not realize, however, was that the "ride" she cheerfully referred to involved towing the house through the Yuculta Rapids, considered one of the most treacherous stretches of water on the coast.

On the morning of their departure, there was plenty of excitement on the dock in Big Bay. Local women appeared with last-minute gifts of freshly baked bread and jars of huckleberry jam, while their husbands stood around shooting the breeze, waiting to say their goodbyes. Then, something happened that was so out of the ordinary that fishermen stopped mending their nets, loggers pushed their hard hats onto the backs of their heads and stared, and for a few minutes all activity and noise on the dock was swept up into an uncanny silence.

Charlie Joe, the ancient and beloved Indigenous Elder who spent his days sitting on the dock chewing tobacco and greeting visitors, stood up and began to walk. Everyone observing this miracle knew that Charlie had not moved in several decades. Every day, all day, he sat on a pile of ropes cushioned with old life jackets, greeting every person who passed by, and he always had tales to tell and plenty of advice to hand out. After all, (he maintained) he was one hundred and eight years old and he knew a thing or two. One of his favourite stories was about the time he saw Christopher Columbus sailing through the Yucultas. Apparently, the *Santa Maria* appeared out of the fog heading straight for the Stuart Island General Store. "Then, *poof!* She was gone," Charlie declared, adding, "I suppose that ol' Mr. Columbus decided to go someplace else to discover our people, even though we didn't need too much help with that kind of thing."

After taking a few breaks to lean against a piling and spit championship streams of tobacco juice into the saltchuck, Charlie reached the end of the dock, stopped in front of my parents' house, now afloat on a bundle of logs, and called for my mother. It was a summons she couldn't ignore, though both she and Dad were anxious to get going before the tide changed. There really wasn't a minute to spare.

Over the thrumming of the tug's engines, Mum didn't catch everything Charlie said; something about a difficult journey, but she shouldn't worry because she and her girls would be safe. Mum thanked Charlie, and he slowly made his way back to his cushioned seat. Everybody on the dock got busy again, including the small group who had come to wave my parents off, yelling last minute pieces of advice like, "Take 'er easy goin' through them rapids." Then the tug pulled away from the dock, towing the little house behind it with my mother and sisters inside.

Dad had been taking boats through the Yucultas since arriving on the coast years earlier, and he was well aware that towing a house through this stretch of water could be like dragging it up and down a flight of stairs a few times over, but the tide was slack and there wasn't much wind so everything was looking good. In no time at all, the tug was churning past the aptly-named Whirlpool Point, about a mile south of Big Bay, steadily moving forward with the house bumping merrily along behind. But suddenly the tug surged forward, and Dad turned to see that the towline had snapped and the house was stalled, almost motionless—before it leaned a little to one side and slipped into a whirlpool.

Mum had been sitting at the kitchen table with Suzy on her lap and Wendy in a playpen, feeling secure that my father was at the helm of their trusty tugboat and he had everything under control. She was enjoying the scenery passing by the window: a waterfall crashing into the inlet, a deer on a bluff, and a particularly beautiful arbutus tree leaning over the water. But then, between spoonfuls of pablum, the house began to tilt and the same scenery kept coming back around: waterfall, deer, arbutus tree, waterfall, deer, arbutus tree, waterfall. . . . Wait a minute! What was happening?

She ran to the window and caught sight of the tug farther away than it should have been before the house pivoted once again and the tug disappeared from view. Meanwhile, Dad watched in horror as the fragile house holding his wife and children appeared to be sinking deeper into the whirlpool with each rotation, but he didn't have time to think about what would happen if it capsized and disappeared altogether. Dashing back into the wheelhouse, he cranked the tug around and began beating back through the rapids, powering past the floundering house before turning the tug around once more and coming alongside the log float. Then things got tricky. In his words, "Everything was goin' real good until that line broke and I had to beat back, then jump from the tug to the float with the line in my hand, and I'm not a real good swimmer. But I knew we could get out of there if I got another line hooked up." And that's exactly what he did. Once they got past Whirlpool Point and were chugging along through also aptly-named, Calm Channel, Mum recalled Charlie's reassuring words and smiled.

Ten years on, Charlie was still sitting on the dock when our family went to Stuart Island to do some shopping and visit friends. Of course, my parents had told me all about him; I had heard his stories and was anxious to meet him, calculating that by now he was one hundred and eighteen years old.

Charlie was obliging when I asked him about Christopher Columbus, and afterwards he asked me the kinds of questions adults always ask kids, like what grade I was in, my age, and did I chew tobacco. I told him I was eight and figured that since our conversation was going in the right direction, I'd ask him how old he was. "Well, I suppose I'm about eighty-nine right about now," he replied. I was dumbfounded and wondered if he said this because he wanted me to think he was merely a spring chicken, or maybe he had forgotten he was the oldest person on earth. Later, I asked Dad why Charlie shaved years off his age, and he told me that Charlie had gone to residential school when he was a kid and hadn't learned much arithmetic there. "His age changes every time I see him," Dad went on. "Maybe it depends on how he feels when he gets up in the morning."

I also asked Dad if he thought Charlie had really seen Christopher Columbus sailing through the Yucultas. He said that he couldn't really say if that were true or not, but since Charlie had been sitting on the dock for so many years, he'd seen many stranger things than Christopher Columbus pass by, especially on Saturday nights when the loggers got their beer delivered from town. "Anyhow," Dad said, "there's nothin' haywire about Charlie. Just ask your mother."

Camp at Fanny Bay

Mistakes do Happen

Mum had done her best to make a home in Fanny Bay.
She hung curtains, hooked rugs, and planted geraniums in coffee cans
on the front porch. And after living there for a few years, the house was
more full of life than ever; Suzy was five years old, Wendy was three,
and I was a baby. Mum and Dad also enjoyed Kurt's company, and my
sisters were always happy to spend time with "Uncle Kurt." He came
for dinner every night, threw Wendy in the air, and played Snakes and
Ladders with Suzy, but he and Dad usually ended up talking about the
price of logs or transmissions, things Mum was not interested in.

She missed the friends she had left behind in Church House. The
ladies there often dropped in for coffee and they laughed and gossiped.
Sometimes she went to Annie Moses's house to sit on the porch and
watch her make baskets. And when Saturday rolled around, a bunch
of them piled into a boat and went to Stuart Island to pick up the mail,
and they often stayed for the dance at the community hall. The loggers
got cleaned up, the women wore dresses, and they danced all night.

Lately, she had caught herself talking to "Jules Verne," the octopus
that lived under the float. She could always spot his pink arms wedged

between the logs, like chewing gum stuck under a table, she thought. But he was a good listener and she talked to him about knitting patterns or the new circle skirts in Eaton's catalogue, that sort of thing. The only problem she had with Jules was that he had a voracious appetite and would not hesitate to steal a full crab trap or a bucket of clams. And one time, as she was bathing Wendy and Suzy in a washtub on the float, she caught him with one of his arms wrapped around a handle of the tub, as if he were about to try and yank it into the water.

Kurt was also feeling the isolation of camp, and after a couple of long winters and five thousand games of Snakes and Ladders, he had begun to suffer from "dental emergencies" that required regular trips to Vancouver. My parents were sympathetic, and my father suggested that since Uncle Kurt would be cooling his heels between dental appointments, he should sign up for lessons at the Arthur Murray Dance Studio. "Women are attracted to men who can dance," Dad told him, "and I should know because that's how I romanced Joan—I took her dancing." Though, in my mother's opinion, he was possibly the worst dancer in Canada.

Uncle Kurt's instructor, Dotty O'Connor, most likely thought that he also was a contender for national recognition, but she too was looking to get married. Her mother had discouraged her interest in becoming an accountant, advising Dotty to "do something pretty. Men like that, especially those big shots with the money. And when the bastards leave, you got something to show for putting up with them, like jewellery or a Cadillac, which will come in real handy," she added, "because I don't want you back here." So, Dotty became a dance instructor, arriving at work each night looking pretty and keeping her eye out for one of those "big shots" her mother talked about. But during the day she did the company's books, something she found deeply satisfying. The numbers fell into place, neat and tidy, and balanced, nothing like her dance partners who couldn't even count to three before stumbling over their own feet—or hers.

For the next year, whenever he was in town, Uncle Kurt took her to The Cave Supper Club where they drank champagne and cha-cha-cha'd until the wee hours. He boasted about having his own logging company and bought her a mink coat, failing to mention that he got it from a guy with a truck full of "unique wholesale items" parked behind the Niagara Hotel.

Returning to camp at the beginning of September 1953, following another "dental emergency," he announced that he and Dotty were married. "She'll be here at the end of the month," he told my parents, "right after her friends at Arthur Murray give her a big send off." With that, he picked up Wendy and waltzed her around the kitchen.

Exactly one month later, Mum was on the float with Suzy and Wendy and me as a Beaver landed offshore. She had been up earlier than usual, made a cake, curled her hair, and was wearing her best apron, the one with yellow roses and no stains. "Okay, girls," she said, "here comes Uncle Kurt's new wife, the lady we've been waiting for all morning," though that wasn't exactly true. Mum had been waiting for Dotty for the last couple of years.

As the plane taxied into the float, she waved to Adam, the pilot. She was always happy to see him whenever he flew into camp to drop off parts or take Uncle Kurt to town. They chatted about their kids who were around the same age, and last time he had even brought a gift for Wendy's birthday, a Rudolph reindeer with a real light in the nose. But today, something was wrong. Adam ignored her, piling out of the cockpit without so much as a hello before opening the passenger door and helping his female passenger onto the float. Only then did he turn to her with a pained smile and said, "Well, Joan, she's all yours." Then he scrambled back into the cockpit, gave her the thumbs up, and took off.

The woman had taken a seat on an overturned washtub and was bent over, holding her head as Mum approached tentatively, taking in the cocktail dress and mink coat. "You're Kurt's wife? Dotty?" Mum asked, hoping she would say she was lost. "Yeah, that's me," the woman answered, lifting her head slowly. "You must be Joan. Nice to meetcha. Didn't he tell you I'd be comin' in today?"

"Well, yes, but I just wanted to make sure there hadn't been a mistake. You know, like you were dropped off in the wrong place. It could happen," Mum replied, "like the time we got the sheep. The freight boat dropped them off, but they should have gone to the Swedes down the inlet. Not that you're anything like a sheep. I'm just making the point, mistakes do happen."

"Oh, you mean this," answered Dotty, standing up with a burst of energy and running her hands down the front of her dress. "I was celebrating. Last chance to have some fun. Didn't get in until the weeeee hours, and there wasn't time to change. Then, I thought, what the hell, might as well arrive in style. So, here I am!"

She began looking around, sobering up as her head turned left, then right, then left again, searching for smokestacks, a sawmill, real houses, not just two shacks on a float.

Too late, she was discovering that her big catch was a big talker. Turning to Mum, she asked, "Where's the camp?"

_\|/_

AS LUCK WOULD HAVE IT, DOTTY'S FIRST WINTER IN HER NEW home was brutally cold. The northeast winds roared up the inlet shaking and rattling the houses around like ice cubes in a Scotch and soda, and logging shut down due to heavy snowfall. Dotty and Uncle Kurt were stuck inside with nothing better to do than "drink too much and act stupid," according to Dad, and Dotty never stopped complaining about living in "the asshole of the world," a phrase Mum hoped Wendy and Suzy wouldn't pick up.

It got so cold that water left in the kitchen sink overnight was frozen solid by morning, and as winter hardened its grip on the shacks, my parents became worried about us kids freezing in our beds at night. Mum decided that the five of us would sleep together in one bed, and every night she "preheated" the icy sheets with flat rocks she had warmed in the oven. Another thing the oven kept toasty warm was me—but not toasted like real toast. Mum didn't put me *in* the oven, she just placed my bassinet near the open oven door to keep me warm.

The optics of this may not have been great, but it worked and I stayed warm. Anyhow, it was around the middle of November of that year Dotty announced she had a baby "in the oven," and she didn't mean her woodstove.

Mum offered Dotty the maternity clothes Aunty Doreen had passed on to her after going five rounds in them before throwing in the towel. There were billowing dresses with Peter Pan collars in cheerful, but faded, prints, and large, large underpants that could be pulled snugly over a big belly, snapping conveniently into place under the wide band of a maternity brassiere. Dotty was horrified, stating, "I'm pregnant, not dead, and that's the only way I'm gonna wear those kinda clothes—if somebody puts them on me in a morgue."

She had none of the robust energy Mum had during her pregnancies. She tired easily, stopped doing housework altogether, and just couldn't face cooking. Even the tiniest whiff of food made her nauseous. As her waistline expanded, she began wearing the "morgue" clothes, but she complained her back was sore and that she wasn't sleeping because the baby kicked all night. Mum was sympathetic. She began cooking for Uncle Kurt and Dotty, and even did their laundry.

In return, Dotty did the bookkeeping for the camp, easily calculating the taxes, stumpage fees, and records of board feet the government required much too often, in my mother's estimation. "I can do that with my eyes closed," she told Mum. "Hand me that pencil, I'm too tired to get up."

She also kept an eye on us girls while Mum did the laundry. I was corralled in a playpen with Wendy to keep me company, Suzy drew pictures of the camp she titled "My AZhol," and Dotty learned that kids sort of took care of themselves. We really weren't much trouble at all, except for the time Suzy made the mistake of calling her "Aunty Dotty" and had to be set straight. "I'm never, ever gonna be an aunty," Dotty patiently explained to Suzy. "You see, aunties never tip bartenders, and they don't wear nice red lipstick like I do. Also . . ." she paused, glancing down at her rotund abdomen, "they wear big underpants when they aren't even pregnant. So, since I do all that other stuff and only wear giant underpants in real tough situations like the one I'm in at the moment, you don't ever hafta call me 'Aunty.' Now, go play." With that problem solved, she continued studying a book called *The Science of Birth* that Kurt had got "wholesale," along with a transistor radio and a Timex watch, from the guy in the truck.

Dotty went into labour the third week of August. "I'm right on the money," she told Mum between contractions, "just like it says in Chapter Nine."

Dad and Uncle Kurt were at work, so Mum called Island Air and helped her pack a suitcase. They walked down to the float to wait for Adam. However, by the time he landed, Dotty had become "overly agitated" (as outlined in Chapter Ten), pacing back and forth on the float, clutching her huge belly, cursing God, her husband, and the un-attractive maternity dress she was wearing. Adam had to load her into the Beaver, feet first, and after slamming the door shut he leaned back against the body of the plane as if he'd just caged a wolverine, prompt-ing my mother to say, "Well, Adam, she's all yours," and she gave him the thumbs up.

Two weeks later, Uncle Kurt and Dotty were back in camp, and before Adam had a chance to tie up, Uncle Kurt swung the passenger door open, shouting, "It's a boy!" Moments later, he was flying down the steps of the plane, holding the baby in one arm and shaking Dad's hand.

"We named him Franky," he announced as Mum and Dad gath-ered round, admiring the baby and congratulating the new parents. "He's a real skookum kid, eh?" Uncle Kurt boasted. "Takes after his old man! A chip off the old block!"

Meanwhile, Dotty, unlike her husband, was remarkably subdued and after a few more words were exchanged about the baby, she picked up her suitcase and walked up to her house.

"Well, isn't that nice," Dad remarked later that night. "That baby has made Kurt and Dot a real nice family." He was sitting on the couch with Suzy and Wendy, about to read them a bedtime story, but before he could turn the first page Mum stopped him.

"He's at least three months old."

"What? How do you know?"

"John. We've had three children. Don't you remember? They were half the size of Franky!"

"Well, they're girls. They're smaller," he answered, looking at my sisters for verification of their petite stature.

"John," she said evenly, "you could dip that kid in bacon grease and leave him on the float overnight and Jules wouldn't go near him. He's way too big for a newborn."

Dad chuckled, ignoring her concern, and turned back to the fairytale.

For the next three days, Mum knocked on Dotty's door. She could hear her talking to Franky and washing dishes, but she wouldn't come to the door. Mum began to get that lonely feeling again and considered talking to Jules, but she thought Dotty might overhear.

On the fourth day, there was a knock on Mum's door, and she opened it to see Dotty in her mink coat and cocktail dress with a bucket of diapers in one hand, Franky in the other, and a basket of dirty laundry at her feet.

"I had nothing else to wear," she said, trying to maintain her composure, "and I only got one clean diaper left and I don't know how to work the washing machine."

"Oh Dot!" Mum said, with relief. "I think you better come in. We'll have a cup of tea."

Dotty dropped the bucket, covered her eyes, and burst into tears. "I was so worried you hated me," she gasped.

Sitting at the kitchen table, she continued to sob, "I'm sorry Joan. I couldn't tell you. I was ashamed."

Over the next hour, interspersed with more tears and nose blowing, the story came out. Dotty explained that when Uncle Kurt had gone to Vancouver a year before for a dentist's appointment and a few drinks at the Niagara. "He only got around to checking off 'a few drinks' from his to-do list. Then a few months later he was back in town again. It was that second molar. You remember?" she asked Mum, who had long ago stopped trying to keep track of Uncle Kurt's teeth and just wanted Dotty to get on with the story. "Anyhow, that's when that bar-maid, Elsie, told him she was pregnant and he was the father.

"I couldn't leave. I had nowhere to go, but then I started to think about how to balance the whole thing out. You know, like credits and debits. We wanted to have kids, that was for sure, so we let Elsie know we'd adopt the baby, and we came up with the fake pregnancy idea because we didn't want anybody to find out. Then, when we got him, he was so big. Kurt said nobody would notice, but I knew you'd figure it out."

Mum reached out and took the baby from Dotty, and sat rocking him for a few minutes before she asked her most pressing question, "Did you use pillows?"

"Only for months five, six, and seven," Dotty replied, matter-of-factly, getting control of herself. After that, I needed something bigger. Like it said in Chapter Nine, so I used the mink, put it in a pillowcase, and it worked out real good."

"Well, Dot," Mum said, taking her friend's hand, "let's go wash those clothes so you got something else to wear besides your best dress, though I do love it. Eaton's catalogue has got one like it but it's got a circle skirt. I'll show you later."

Suzy, me, Wendy. Fanny Bay.

Character Building

WHEN SUZY TURNED SIX, MUM AND DAD SENT HER TO PRINCESS Louisa's School for Girls on Vancouver Island. It was a boarding school, much the same as every other soul-crushing educational institution of its kind. Students were moulded into obedient, well-mannered children who wouldn't know how to have fun even if they fell into a barrel of monkeys, which was highly unlikely and probably not much fun, but you get the point. Of course, my young parents didn't know anything about boarding schools, or soul-crushing for that matter. They just wanted Suzy to have the best education possible.

Dad and Uncle Kurt logged from March through to November, then it was time to hunker down in their derelict floathouses to wait for spring. Mum and Dotty rationed canned food and other dry goods they'd put aside for the months freight boats didn't deliver to the coastal communities, and Dad and Uncle Kurt fished and chopped wood for the stoves. They got by until 1955, when all hope of making a better life for themselves took a turn for the worse, because hope can do that, veer right off track.

That year, my father and uncle had once again failed to get a timber licence of their own, and they ended up working for Uncle Harold, who had come to be known as "That Sonofabitch," not only to his immediate family, but to almost every logger on the coast. He ran his logging shows with antiquated, busted-up machinery and paid his men next to nothing.

At first, Mum homeschooled Suzy; there was no other choice. She had sent away to the Ministry of Education for teaching materials, and it wasn't long before a thick package arrived in the mail containing several booklets, each one emphasizing a skill the average six-year-old should "acquire competency in within a reasonable range of ability." There were booklets on penmanship, science, reading, music, phonics, calisthenics, and arithmetic. Mum was soon overwhelmed. She didn't have enough time to teach Suzy because she was also taking care of Wendy and me, keeping the woodstove going, hauling buckets of water from the creek, and washing the laundry by hand. Besides, what the hell were "phonics"?

My parents decided the only solution was to send Suzy to boarding school; they just had to find the money to pay for it. Night after night, they sat at their kitchen table pencilling calculations on scraps of paper and forecasting optimistic profits for the following year, but it was never enough. The only thing to do was borrow the money from "That Sonofabitch."

Dad rowed down the inlet to Uncle Harold's camp, and after pleasantries were exchanged over cups of watery coffee and slivers of stale pie, Uncle Harold said he'd be more than happy to lend my father the money for Suzy's tuition. Then he pulled out a notebook, opened it to a new page, and pushed it across the table to Dad, saying, "You write the date and the amount here and sign your name to make things all legal so's I don't have to come after you with a bunch of them bigshot lawyers to get my money back." Dad did as instructed, then returned the notebook to Uncle Harold who added his signature to the paper with a large X. It was clear that even though Uncle Harold was illiterate, he was a shrewd businessman.

Now that the tuition money was guaranteed, Mum wasted no time writing to Princess Louisa's, and a month later she received a reply from the school's headmistress, Miss Scallion. Her letter was brief and to the point, stating that Princess Louisa's "would entertain" the idea of accepting Suzy for September. Mum and Dad just had to present themselves at the school for an interview to determine Suzy's "suitability." Dad figured he and Mum had been invited to a party for parents of potential students since the letter had stated the school "would entertain." However, several weeks later, when they were sitting on hard chairs in Miss Scallion's office, they didn't feel "entertained" in the least, though they remained optimistic about Suzy's "suitability."

The headmistress asked if Suzy knew her shapes and colours. Could she recite the alphabet? The Lord's Prayer? Nursery rhymes? God Save the Queen? "Yes, yes, yes, she can do all that," Mum and Dad answered confidently. "Does she wet the bed? Bite? Kick? Faint?" they were asked. "No, no, no, she doesn't do any of that," my parents replied with enthusiasm. "Does she know her manners?" "Yes! All of them!" Mum and Dad almost shouted. They were sure Suzy was an ideal candidate for this fancy-schmancy school. Then Miss Scallion asked, "Of course she rides, doesn't she?" Mum and Dad were confused. Rides? Rides what? Their minds were racing. The only thing to ride in a logging camp was a boat. Did that count? Did "ride" mean ride a bicycle? That must be it, but there were no bicycles in camp. . . . "What exactly do you mean by 'ride'?" Dad asked. "Horses of course," sniffed the headmistress. "All the girls here ride; it's part and parcel of the curriculum." Dad didn't know what a curriculum was, and he had already been tricked by the gobbledegook of Miss Scallion's letter stating that there was going to be a party despite there not being a balloon or beer in sight. "Well," he replied, "Suzy hasn't ridden too many horses, but if the horses have to carry parcels of that curriculum you mentioned, I'm sure she'll pitch in and help."

Suzy was dropped off at Princess Louisa's in early September 1955.

Soon after, she developed pneumonia and was left in the school infirmary to recover. Lying on her bed, day after day, she made friends with a crack in the ceiling that resembled a rabbit. It was the only company she had.

When Dad arrived at the school to pick her up for the Christmas holidays, he found her sitting alone on a bench outside Miss Scallion's office. She was wearing every article of clothing she owned: wooly knee socks, a kilt, a cardigan, a school blazer, a duffle coat, a tam pulled down over her ears, and six pairs of underpants for good measure. She was red in the face and sweating buckets. Dad asked her why she hadn't taken off her coat if she were so hot, and Suzy replied, "Headmistress says we need to keep warm or we might get sick again and if that happens, it will be our own fault."

It didn't take long for my father to find out from the chatty school secretary that pneumonia had swept through the school, leaving several girls bedridden for weeks. Leaning across her desk and looking both ways, she whispered to Dad, "The doctor hit the roof and wrote the headmistress a letter saying he could shut the school down because the students were 'compelled to participate in activities counterintuitive to good health,' which I figure was a real nice way of saying that she had better stop making the girls take cold showers every morning and swim in that outdoor pool, even when it was raining. And another thing," she whispered, "at night, they were sleeping with them windows in the dormitory wide open. Headmistress called it 'character building,' but I don't think it was right."

Confronted by Dad, Miss Scallion became even more condescending than she had been at the "suitability" interview. With a pained look on her face, she momentarily closed her eyes, then slowly and patiently explained to my father that challenges were to be welcomed because they taught the girls how to deal with adversity. In return, my father gave Miss Scallion the kind of look he gave a rotten hemlock before he took a power saw to it, then he mustered all of his own patience and quietly said, "I'll be taking my daughter home now," and in no time at all, he and Suzy were on a bush plane flying back into camp. Later that

Fill'er Up, Princess!

BY 1957, DAD AND UNCLE KURT FINALLY HAD THEIR OWN LOGG-
ing show and were making enough money to pay their crew and, occasionally, pay themselves. However, they were embroiled in a dispute
with Uncle Harold over some logging equipment he had leased to
them, which he guaranteed was in good working order when it was
neither good, nor working. My father and Uncle Kurt wanted their
money back, and they knew the only way to do that was to sue.

Their lawyers thought about the case long enough to justify a hefty
bill, then they wrote the following letter.

September 9, 1957

Messrs. K.H. Wankel
J.B. Willcock
Willcock & Wankel, Logging Ltd.
Postmaster, Stuart Island, B.C.

Dear Sirs:

We have carefully considered the
information given to us by you, and in our opinion,
if you went to trial, you could not recover any
money, nor can you avoid paying Mr. Stearman the
amount he is claiming.

You will note that the net profit made
by your company in the year ending December 31st,
1956 was $16,524.16, as shown in Exhibit "A" and
the rental of the equipment from Mr. Stearman
was $15,024.60, as shown in Exhibit "B", leaving
your company a net profit of $1,499.56, as shown in
Exhibit "C".

In view of all the circumstances, it is our
opinion that you should settle this dispute with Mr.
Stearman and accept the amount shown on Exhibit
"C" minus our legal fees, yet to be determined.

Could we hear from you in this regard at
your earliest convenience?

Yours very truly,

Badner, Lowes, Badner & Edwin

After the legal fees were paid, my parents had $3.56 in the bank,
which was about three dollars more than Uncle Kurt and Dotty had.
The remaining company assets were sold off, and by the end of the year
my father and uncle got just enough money to rent houses in North
Vancouver and open up a gas station on Kingsway Avenue in Vancouver.
They had convinced themselves they no longer wanted to be loggers and
were confident the gas station would be a real money-maker because
1950s cars got few miles per gallon and had gas tanks the size of ele-
phants' back ends.

Besides, owning a gas station was not such a bad job. All you had
to do was pump gas and fiddle with car engines, and you didn't have to
build your own road to get to work because it had already been done
for you. Plus, the new Second Narrows Bridge was under construction.
It was going to have six lanes spanning Burrard Inlet, bring even more
customers to the station, and get Dad and Uncle Kurt to work and back
home again in the wink of an eye. Things were not so bad after all, until

they were, as in national disaster, bad.

On June 17 the following year, around 4:30 pm, Dad finished work for the day, hopped in his Chevy, drove down Kingsway, turned onto Hastings Street, and approached the Second Narrows Bridge. As usual, he could see two bridges up ahead: the original bridge he was about to drive over and the new, and as yet incomplete, bridge towering beside it. But there were cop cars and ambulances blocking the road, and he was horrified to see that two massive spans of the new bridge had collapsed into the inlet, leaving a framework of bent steel girders hanging over the water.

Later, when the shock had worn off, my father and uncle anticipated a return to business as usual, but the bridge collapse had impacted business on Kingsway Avenue, and the flow of cars pulling into the gas station had become a mere trickle. It was clear the partners were going broke again. But just as they were about to board up the station, the police arrived and told them to hold off. It was a matter of utmost importance concerning Queen and country—sort of. Princess Margaret was about to visit Vancouver as part of her royal tour of Canada, and her motorcade was scheduled to drive down Kingsway Avenue. The RCMP wanted Dad and Uncle Kurt to keep the station open in the event of anything going wrong with the princess's car. Loyal subjects that they were, my father and uncle agreed and cleaned the station from top to bottom, polishing the pumps and giving the "Ladies" a once-over in case Her Royal Highness might need a moment or two on the throne. Aunty Margy, who read all the trashy magazines and knew exactly what was going on behind closed doors at Buckingham Palace, said the princess was a real boozehound and would only stop at the station if Dad put a big sign out front that read, "Scotch Whisky, Half Price."

When the big day finally arrived, Mum, Suzy, Wendy, and I, along with several aunts, uncles and cousins, lined up on the sidewalk in front of the station to await Her Royal Highness's arrival. It didn't take long before we heard motorcycles approaching, then several large convertibles appeared. This was the moment! Was Princess Margaret of the House of Windsor, sister to the Queen, and all-round fun party girl going to make a pit stop at our station? I had my fingers crossed, wishing for a flat tire, a full bladder, anything to make her pull over.

Later, I could only recall a convertible whizzing by in a blur, and a glimpse of a gloved hand in the air. Then she was gone, and Dad and Uncle Kurt were not far behind. They decided to go back up the coast and "give 'er" one more time in a place called Orford Bay, way up Bute Inlet.

Chapter Six

Summer Camp

The versatility of a breadbox, learning a second language, and cocktail hour in Orford Bay.

"Hold on, girls!"

ON THE FIRST DAY OF JULY, LONG BEFORE THE SUN WAS UP, OUR house in North Vancouver was abuzz with activity. Mum ran from room to room latching windows and drawing curtains, while Suzy, Wendy, and I squeezed last minute items into suitcases that were already brimming with books, baseball mitts, bathing suits, and a jack-knife for each of us since Mum hated it when we borrowed hers. This is how it was whenever we went to Orford Bay. There was a ferry to catch to Vancouver Island, some driving to do, and reservations on a bush plane that was scheduled to take off later that day—with or without us.

We couldn't have been happier to be leaving the suburbs behind. Certainly, our middle-class life was comfortable in the extreme, but that was only the half of it. We lived a separate life up the coast and, to be honest, it was preferable to the scheduled and predictable existence we had in town.

During the school year, my mother did her best to guide my sisters and me down a path of compliance to ensure that we "fit in." We were registered for lessons in which we had no interest: piano for me and "Young Ladies Etiquette" for Suzy, while Wendy racked up a string of Girl Guide badges, including one for knot-tying, a skill useful only to the likes of Ferdinand Magellan. We also were taught to sit up straight in church, never laying ourselves out on a pew to suck the Skippy peanut butter from under our fingernails like the Reid children did, just as our minister was coming to the part in the sermon about God's love and how we were all fairly undeserving in that department.

At school, Miss Mackenzie, our guidance counsellor, became concerned about my sisters and me after finding out that our father did "physical labour." Pulling us aside every now and then, she offered words of encouragement about how we could "rise above our environment." We shrugged her off, aware she was offering us a version of her own life—safe and boring.

Aunty Doreen summed up the general anesthesia of our suburban culture by saying that if her family were swept over Niagara Falls, "I could depend on a sales lady at the village dress shop to say, 'I suppose you'll be wanting a black dress then. We just got some lovely ones in,' and that would be the end of it, other than a condolence card with a coupon for 10% off my next purchase."

Once the luggage was stowed in the trunk of the Chevy, and Suzy had run back into the house three times to grab books she couldn't live without, we piled into the car. Wendy and Suzy stood in the back seat, while I took up a horizontal position in the rear window. In the driver's seat, Mum checked her lipstick in the rear-view mirror, donned her sunglasses, and shouted, "Hold on, girls!" And we took off.

We had not seen Dad in five months because, like all camp bosses, he never left camp during logging season. Ever. He knew that if he did, the minute he got to town he'd get a call from Orford Bay, and it wasn't going to be a social call from the guys wishing him a swell vacation. No, the logger on the other end of the line was going to tell him there had been a machinery breakdown and the parts couldn't be flown in for five days, so camp was shut down, and that the loggers he was paying twenty-five dollars a day were sitting around complaining about how guys at a camp up the inlet had their own ping-pong table, or the cook had quit, or Vince, the chokerman, had cut his hand "real bad" and was in hospital in Campbell River, or the road had washed out again, or, well, a million bad things could happen if you had any wise ideas about taking a few days off. So Dad stayed put in Orford Bay, which didn't mean that bad stuff didn't happen when he was in camp, but at least he was there to try and get things up and running again when everything went to hell.

Approaching the ferry terminal at Horseshoe Bay, Mum barely slowed down to buy a ticket before rocketing into the cavernous hold of the ship and braking hard, sending Suzy and Wendy lurching over the front seat before ricocheting backwards to crash into me as I rolled out of the back window.

Undeterred, we tumbled out of the car and took the stairs to the upper decks two at a time, racing to get a window seat in the dining room. Those were the days when travellers dressed up, including the Willcock girls. We showed up on the ferry every year in matching ensembles Mum had made. Her most noteworthy creations included three pairs of hot pink palazzo pants with legs wide enough to fit an African elephant, topped off with hand knit sweaters, long in the arm and short in the body. We looked like a family of pink pachyderms.

But all self-consciousness was put aside as we slid into a banquette and a waiter materialized, wearing an Eton jacket and bow tie, and graciously handed us menus sticky with syrup. Breakfast was served before we even left the dock, giving the kitchen and dining room staff time to serve meals, clean up, and prep for the next onslaught of customers before the ferry docked in Nanaimo. In a flash, our waiter was back with half a dozen plates running up one arm and down the other. There were mountains of bacon, a dozen fried eggs slipping around a plate, towers of toast, and stacks of pancakes. But we didn't dig in. Nope. We carefully covered every plate and glass on the table with napkins and waited for the ferry to pull away from the dock in a series of shakes and shudders that brought down asbestos particles from the ceiling insulation. Nobody complained. It was part of the dining experience—bacon and eggs with a sprinkling of asbestos.

Docking in Nanaimo, Mum roared off the ferry like she'd just robbed a bank. We flew north along the Island Highway, passing the small towns of Parksville and Courtenay in a blur, heading straight for the airport in Campbell River, where we skidded sideways across the parking lot, coming to a halt directly in front of the terminal. Taking a calming breath, Mum reapplied her lipstick and stepped out of the car, then turned back to us, saying, "Hold on, girls, I'll just let them know we are here. Right on time, as usual."

Low Tide

Orford River sandbars

THE FIRST THING WE KIDS WANTED TO DO WHEN WE GOT TO camp was to go play with Franky on the sandbars at the mouth of the Orford River. At low tide, we ran and cartwheeled on the vast expanse of sand fanning out from the mouth of the river, built roadways and spillways, and chased each other with dead salmon. It was fun and free and wild, and getting there and back was part of the adventure.

Leaving camp, we trekked along the shoreline for half a mile before dropping down onto a saltwater marsh of sharp-edged seagrass, following a path engineered by a consortium of otters that had scant respect for straight lines. Squelching through the tall grass, we were on high alert for suspicious rustlings on either side of the path, each of us silently worrying that a bear might be nearby. But the camp dog, Smokey, was with us and as long as he stayed calm, we did too.

About halfway across the marsh, a ridiculously small floathouse blocked the way. It had arrived in Orford Bay on a stormy night a few years back, and since that time nobody had come looking for their house, so here it sat. It would have been adorable for its dollhouse dimensions had it not had such a disturbing history.

It was easier to scramble through the house, climbing up onto the log float, entering the back door and exiting through the front window, than to follow the slimy otter path that dove beneath it, which was exactly what Smokey did, emerging slick with muck and smelling of low tide. I never liked being inside the house. It was a mouldering mausoleum containing all the earthly belongings of a man named Ivan Solberg, right down to a made-up bed, now dank and musty, a rusting alarm clock, and one mildewed slipper. We learned the man's name from the uncashed cheques he had left behind, some made out to him from the government of Canada, others from logging companies none of us had ever heard of. The kitchen cupboards held bloated cans of food and pots and pans, rusted and filthy with mouse droppings, while the linoleum floor, once a jolly red and white checkerboard, was lifting up in the corners, exposing rotten floorboards.

There were also letters from a woman named Aase. They weren't in English but the handwriting was beautiful, her clear signature followed by X's and O's. And, in a kitchen drawer, we found black and white photos, the old kind with ruffled edges, showing a woman with a baby, a child with a dog, and a couple smiling into the camera as they waltzed around a room decorated with paper streamers. I wondered what made Ivan Solberg leave everything behind and move to this small house in the wilderness, eventually letting it go too, untethered and tossed about with no direction.

Out of the house and back on the otter path, we could smell the salt in the air and hear the river echoing off the cliffs. As we got closer, the seagrass thinned out and we splashed through freshwater creeks running into the ocean and saltwater channels flowing in the opposite direction. Stepping over rusting boom chains and lengths of wire rope embedded in the sand, we skirted the grassy finger of land where Dad shot the grizzly after it tore the door off the cookhouse. Then a few hundred yards further, the sandbars stretched out before us like untouched canvases, smooth and clean, and we could do as we pleased for a few hours until the tide raced back into the bay.

We played tag, scratched out giant hopscotch games in the wet sand, and wrote the names of the boys or girls we loved in big letters, stubbing them out before anybody could see. Here and there, water-logged tree stumps dotted the sandbars, black with seaweed and mussels, too slippery to climb but excellent backdrops for games requiring a haunted house or a petrified forest.

The river roared nearby, a milky turquoise, beautiful and dangerous. We knew enough to stay away from the soft shoulders that could shrug at the smallest provocation, sending us into the torrent.

When the salmon were spawning, the sand was littered with dead coho, their hooked noses and sharp teeth giving them the appearance of old men. And, of course, it was the salmon that attracted the grizzlies. They fished along the banks, leaving behind paw prints the size of dinner plates. Whenever I found a set of prints, I would stick my fingers into the depths of the claw marks, trying to determine how long they were, but I never reached the bottom of a single one. I'm not sure why our parents let us play in an area now considered one of the best places on earth for viewing grizzlies, but we were never afraid. However, if Smokey ever stopped dead, stared into the bush along the shoreline, and began to growl, we knew it was time to get home, fast.

One day, Wendy forgot her sweater over by the river and Mum made her go back and get it before the tide swept it away. She rushed back, thinking she knew where the sweater was, but she was mistaken and criss-crossed the sandbars several times before she found it, floating in the shallows, just as it was getting dark. By the time she turned back towards camp, the tide was rushing across the sand and she ran as fast as she could, glancing back every few minutes at the petrified stumps, which had taken on grizzly silhouettes. Arriving back in camp, soggy sweater in hand and out of breath, Wendy found Mum waiting for her on the beach, the fear obvious on both their faces.

Our adventures always ended with Franky shouting, "We gotta go!" as the tide stealthily ran across the sand, coming in fast. Sometimes, leaving too late, we had to make a run for it and ended up wading through the marsh grass with water swirling higher and higher around our legs, and we had to grab Smokey by the scruff of the neck and pull him along. Then Ivan's house appeared, and we clambered through the kitchen window and out the back door, dog in hand, onward to camp until the next low tide.

Endless Possibilities

THE BEACH AT ORFORD BAY WAS NEVER GOING TO BE FEATURED on a glossy wall calendar. In fact, it barely qualified as a beach at all having only about ten grains of sand, with the remainder of the sea-shore carpeted in a mudflat, reeking and littered with debris. This was a cold, mean place, battered by winds off the river on one side and shadowed by mountains on the other. You couldn't walk here without experiencing some sort of calamity: boots sucked off in the mud, fingers torn on broken glass, legs entangled in twisted fishing line. But this expanse of muck was pure magic for us kids, and digging in the mud or wading through murky tidal pools we always found something fascinating.

Well, let me clarify: not all of us were racing to the beach. Suzy and I were fair-weather explorers, staying at home on rainy days pulled up close to the woodstove with books and magazines in hand while Wendy and Franky burst out of the front door, unzipped raincoats flying behind them as they sprinted to the beach. Later, I'd watch them from the kitchen window, bent over, heads together, examining some new discovery they'd yanked out of the mud. I wished I was made of sturdier stuff, but then the lure of a *Nancy Drew* called me back.

However, when the sun came out, the beach was irresistible. There were bright orange sea stars to admire, their long legs draped over rocks like worn-out showgirls, geoducks squirting water into the air, and ravens strutting around as if they owned the place. As we turned over rocks, armies of speckled crabs, each no bigger than a thumbprint, greeted us, raising their pincers defiantly before scuttling for cover. They dined on waterlogged lettuce, soggy orange peels, tea bags, and other delicacies from the cookhouse garbage that was dumped into the deepest part of the bay every night and washed ashore each morning. It was also fun to run at full speed across the slick muck, then put the brakes on and slide as if we were ice-skating, or take a length of bull kelp, the kind with bulbous heads, whip it overhead lasso-style and send it flying. On the south side of the bay, we played tag beneath a rotten logging trestle from a half century before, racing between the bow-legged pylons that staggered across the beach, coated in a psoriatic mess of mussels and peeling lichen.

Besides the trestle, there was plenty of other evidence of human history on the beach. Shards of blue and white porcelain were reminders of the Chinese who hand-logged the Orford Valley around the turn of the century. Bits of crockery with images of willow trees, pagodas, turtles, and laughing deities were like pieces of a jigsaw puzzle, fragments of bigger stories. My favourite was of a woman standing on a bridge that curved like an eyebrow. I imagined a Chinese logger gazing at this image on the side of his teacup, hoping the woman he loved was waiting for him back home. I didn't know if loggers had romantic yearnings of this sort, but I was sure these men must have been lonely.

More common beach finds were chunks of sturdy hotelware, the kind used in all logging camps at the time. The plates and mugs were glazed an institutional white with dark green lines circling inside the rims to let cooks know where the limits of their generosity should end. Other debris was useful when it came to constructing sand (mud) castles: bullet casings became cannons, the long necks of beer bottles created ideal turrets, and the sole of a caulk boot made a dandy studded castle door. Tin cans were useless and creepy because there was often a slimy creature moving around inside, though Franky did find that Campbell Soup cans fit him like a glove, so to speak. He would slip his hand inside a rusty can and pretend he was Arnie Johansson, the old logger who sat outside the store at Shoal Bay and loved to tell anybody who would listen the story of how his hand was pinched off between two logs. The retelling of Arnie's story never got old for Franky either, until the day he couldn't get his hand out of a can; the lid was still partially attached and pushed inside, and the more he pulled on the can, the deeper the jagged lid dug into the back of his hand.

Coming to his rescue, Wendy and I vigorously pushed and pulled on the can while Franky yelled about how much it hurt and how stupid we were. *We* were the stupid ones? I figured he was going to end up like Arnie Johansson if we didn't get the can off his hand, but Franky escaped and took off up the beach, bursting through our front door a few minutes later screaming, "Aunty Joan, Aunty Joan, it's stuck, it's stuck!" while waving his soup can hand around and splattering muck and blood all over the kitchen floor. Mum looked at her previously clean floor, looked at Franky dancing around, and sighed. "Okay, Franky, come here and let's see what you've done this time," she said, as she gently pushed the sides of the corroded can close together and his hand slipped out. What an idiot.

There were other castoffs on the beach that even Franky stayed away from, like all the food the cook threw out. No electricity in camp meant no refrigeration, and cases of rotting pork chops littered the beach, along with roasts of beef tinged iridescent green and bloated chicken carcasses so full of bugs they looked as if they could get up and dance. Of course, the eagles loved these kinds of meals. They could skip the hassle of hunting and just eat to their heart's content. It was fast food for predators.

Occasionally, we'd come across a dead seal lying in the mud with its nose cut off, a victim of a Fisheries Department program offering a few bucks for each seal nose they received since it was a scientific fact that seals decreased fish stocks. This was an offer some of the loggers in camp could not refuse, and on summer nights they borrowed the camp rifle and went out in a speedboat to shoot seals and slice off their noses, preserving the booty in jars of kerosene until it could be redeemed for cash.

The beach was also a virtual logging museum. Rusting heaps of machinery from the early days of the industry lay scattered across the mudflats. When we walked there with Dad, he'd tell us stories about some of the equipment, like the old steam donkeys. "Jeez, that's a real old one. We had these in the thirties. They broke down all the time, and I remember an old Swede crying after about the tenth breakdown. I was only fifteen and had never seen one of those tough old buggers cry. I didn't know what to do." Then he'd give the rusting skeleton a few nudges with the toe of his boot and go on, "The crew who left this donkey here probably went belly up and walked away. They didn't have the money to get their equipment towed out of here, which was too bad because a donkey like this was a big improvement on horse logging. You know," he went on, "your Uncle Harold started out horse logging in the twenties. He was working up in Jervis Inlet for a while, and after that logging show went belly up, they left the horses behind. I went back there a few years ago, and there were horse bones all over the beach. I guess they didn't have enough to eat."

When the tide was out, we could walk down the beach almost to the mouth of the bay, and from this vantage point, it was easy to spot the killer whales on the far side of the inlet. They always appeared at the end of August, surging north towards the head of Bute Inlet, their dorsal fins rising and falling in torrents of white water. Then one day a fisherman who dropped into camp for coffee told us he'd spotted an albino killer whale at the south end of the inlet. He told us to be on the lookout for it because the whales would be going past our camp in a day or two. And sure enough, a few days later it appeared, its white fin rising out of the water in the middle of the pack. We stood watching the whales until the tide started coming in, sweeping in new possibilities for the next time we raced down to the beach.

Bazooka!

IT WAS STILL DARK WHEN DAD WENT OUT ONTO THE PORCH, BENT down to find his boots, and came face to face with a grinning visitor. Startled, he jumped back, making sure his eyes weren't playing tricks on him. Then he gingerly reached out and picked up the human skull that had seemingly materialized out of the ether. "Jesus Christ!" he said, not in the nice way our creator is called upon to bless the dearly departed, but in the pissed-off way, because he knew the RCMP had to be notified. They would fly into camp, shut down logging for a week and question each and every resident of Orford Bay (all ten of us) to find out if we had noticed that anybody had gone missing. Dad went back inside, handed the skull to my gob-smacked mother, and said, "If it's not washed-out roads and flat tires, it's a goddamn skull. I guess you gotta call the RCMP," and he left for work.

Not knowing the right protocol for storing human skulls, Mum plonked it down on the kitchen table; she would think about a good place for it later. Then she turned on the radio telephone and tried to get a call through to the RCMP in Campbell River. However, the lines were more staticky than usual that morning, and the louder Mum shouted at the operator to connect her to "the police...! the police...! the POLICE!!!" the louder the testy operator shouted back, "Madam! You can say 'please' as many times as you like, but I cannot clearly make out the name of who it is you wish to call. You'll have to try again later," and she ended the call.

Meanwhile, the racket woke me and my sisters. We got up, wandered into the kitchen, and sat down at the table, which had been set with the usual breakfast items: milk, cereal, toast, and something altogether new, a human skull. This was fantastic and arguably the most exciting thing to happen in Orford Bay since the deer ran through the clothesline and got Uncle Kurt's long johns caught on its antlers. (He chased the deer all over camp trying to get his underwear back, which he eventually did, though the antlers had poked lots of holes in them.) However, this skull was a totally different matter. It was a genuine mystery and would require the combined detective skills of us three girls to figure out who had lost their head.

Suzy, the mature one, deduced that since nobody had been reported missing from the bunkhouse, and the cook had been seen that morning, we could eliminate anyone in camp as the actual owner of the skull. Furthermore, we all agreed that Smokey was the likely skull snatcher. He frequently brought old deer bones back to camp and dropped them on the porch to show off before burying them. So the skull could have come from anywhere in the Orford Valley because Smokey was like a virtual Texas Ranger when it came to covering territory. The only place he couldn't get to was the far side of the river because the current was too strong.

I thought the skull could have been brought into camp by the weird logger who never spoke—except to himself. I reminded my sisters that he had a picture of his girlfriend beside his bed but he never got any letters from her. "So, she's probably dead, and we are looking at her right now," I concluded with not a little satisfaction in the realization that having read fourteen *Nancy Drew* books in a row had paid off.

Wendy disagreed, however, saying that the skull had to be that of the last cook we had, and I had to admit she had a point. He was the worst cook ever, couldn't even make scrambled eggs, so maybe the loggers had murdered him. Then Wendy drove her point home. Looking around the table at Suzy and me, she asked, "Did either of you see him get on a plane out of here?" We slowly shook our heads no. "I didn't either," she whispered, and took a big slug of orange juice, then slammed her glass down on the table making the skull wobble up and down in agreement.

On and on we went, growing increasingly detailed and macabre until Franky arrived for a late breakfast and shattered all our theories. Picking the skull up, he examined it like a regular Sherlock, then smugly announced that it obviously belonged to a caveman. He pointed out that there were no fillings in the teeth, and he should know about fillings since he had about twenty of them in his mouth from chewing Bazooka bubble gum every single day and never brushing his teeth. And, he went on, since cavemen didn't chew bubble gum, they didn't get cavities, which proved the skull belonged to a caveman. Case closed.

Turning to Mum, we began badgering her with questions about the skull, but she wasn't listening. She just sat there with her hand over her mouth in a shocked and confused sort of way. Then she picked the skull up and put it in the breadbox, all the while telling us we should show some respect, we were ghoulish, and we should stop with all the wild stories because we didn't have a clue about where the skull had come from. "As soon as your father gets home, we will figure out what to do," she announced with determination, though she still looked rattled as she ordered Smokey out of the house. He had been pacing around the kitchen furtively eyeing the skull, trying to look as if he didn't want to snatch it and take off. After he left, Mum took over pacing duties, walking round the kitchen and opening the breadbox every few minutes to make sure the skull was still there.

When Dad got home, Mum met him on the front porch, and they had a brief one-sided conversation (my mother being the one side), and a decision was made to ask an authority on human heads, and bones, and dead people in general, about the identity of the skull. The problem was that we were short on authorities in camp on pretty much every subject you could think of. Mum and Dad thought about asking the cook, but he never really dealt with heads of any type except for fish, and the loggers who liked to hunt usually shot deer so they only knew about heads with antlers. Then there were the ex-cons. They were probably the best ones to ask, but nobody really wanted to hear what they knew about this particular subject.

It finally came down to the self-proclaimed smart guy and number one most useless logger in camp, the university student who had been hired for the summer. When the smart guy picked up the skull, he immediately starting talking—a lot. "This is at least one hundred years old, maybe older," he declared, and commenced to drone on about how "it could be from one of the Spanish explorers of Bute Inlet in the 1700s, or maybe it's one of those Canadian Pacific Railroad engineers who were going to create the terminus of the railroad up at the head of the inlet, or maybe it's a fisherman, or one of the Chinese who apparently logged. . . ."

Dad cut him off and asked how he knew the skull was over a hundred years old. "Oh, that's easy," answered the brainy university student. "My father's a dentist. Look at the teeth in this skull. They're perfect, no cavities, no missing teeth. This person didn't eat a lot of refined sugars. Ergo, he or she probably died a long time ago, before people ate tons of candy, and drank pop, and chewed bubble gum. When I was a kid, my parents never let me eat any sugary stuff, and I have perfect teeth, but I was never allowed to go to birthday parties because of all the cake and candy, and I was quite lonely as a child and. . . ." Again, Dad cut in. "Right," he said as he directed the brainy guy out the door, "that's real interesting. So, nothing to worry about. This skull is old and the RCMP don't give a damn about a guy who died long before there were liquor stores to hold up."

The skull stayed put, and Mum told us kids not to fool around with it but, when she wasn't around, we encouraged every logger who dropped in for a visit to help themselves to a piece of cake from the breadbox.

A few months later when a Columbia Coast Mission boat arrived in Orford Bay, we finally said goodbye to our bonehead friend. The Coast Mission ships were floating churches, serving the camps and reserves on the coast. Mum gave the skull to Reverend Green, the ship's Anglican minister. "I could tell he didn't really want it," Mum told us later. "I think he didn't know what to do with it. I told him about our breadbox and he said it wasn't the first place he would have considered but he'd give it some thought. Anyhow, he's going to make arrangements for a proper interment."

We never did figure out where Smokey had found the skull, and he never brought us any of its corresponding parts. Things in camp returned to normal, though Franky wouldn't let the story go. He continued to remind everyone—a lot—about how he solved the mystery, long before the smart guy, simply by chewing Bazooka bubble gum. "Ergo," he didn't have to go to university to become smart, because he already was.

Me with the skull.

Won't that be Fun!

EVERY SUMMER FLOTILLAS OF AMERICAN YACHTS SAILED NORTH to British Columbia to enjoy the natural beauty of the coast. They cruised the inlets by day and tied up to camp floats in the early evening, sometimes even venturing ashore to take photos of "American eagles" and "real lumberjacks." For Wendy, Franky, and me, the boaters were representative of all things good about Americans: they were friendly and generous and possessed all the latest gadgets from cameras to fishing rods to popcorn machines. They also gave us a break from regular camp life, and we found them to be as charming and peculiar as they found us.

The majority of the yachts were Chris Crafts, perfect examples of American style and workmanship, and also dandy status symbols, since Elvis and Frank Sinatra each owned one. They were also immaculate from stem to stern, with well-oiled decks, polished brass bits, and sparkling white hulls. And the visitors themselves were also sparkling white, from their pale complexions to their linen cruise wear, exemplifying American confidence and success from head to toe. And, just in case anybody had doubts about where they were from, bedsheet-size American flags fluttered off the stern of every vessel.

Without fail, boaters arriving in Orford Bay motored over to where Uncle Floyd was working on the boom and received his standard "meet and greet." No, they could not tie up to the boom unless they wanted to wake up in Vancouver because that's where the logs were headed. Yes, they could tie up to the big float across the bay. Yes, he was a real lumberjack. No, they could not take his picture. No, he did not want a real American cigarette. After that, the drama of tying up ensued, and it was always painful to watch—and listen to—because securing a spiffy clean yacht to a log float coated in black oil and held together with rusty boom chains can be tricky.

First, there was the careful placement of bumpers about every six inches along the hull to protect it from rubbing against the float. Then the shouting began. Frustrated captains yelled orders like, "Fer Chrissakes, Dolores! I said reverse!" followed by mutinous retorts along the lines of, "Keep your shirt on, Larry! If you wanted someone who understood all these fucking dials, maybe you should've asked Buzz Aldrin to be your first mate!"

Once a boat docked and everyone had their shirts back on, Franky and Wendy and I leaped into our speedboat and raced towards the foreign vessel at top speed, maxing out the capability of our Seagull outboard motor at six knots. Our mission was to get the Yanks to hand over what they called "candy bars." First, we had to answer the question Americans have been asking kids the world over since they first began trying to convert others to the joys of junk food and capitalism: "Have you kids ever had an American candy bar?" We sadly shook our heads no, (not letting on we had been gorging on American chocolate all summer), and soon the Babe Ruths and 3 Musketeers were flying through the air into our greedy little hands. Of course, Franky, who was not afraid of risking the loss of his soul to the eternal fires of hell, told the Yanks exactly what they wanted to hear, like where the fifty-pound salmon were biting or the best place to spot a mother grizzly with eighteen of her adorable cubs. He was always rewarded with a deluge of "candy bars"—and he never shared.

One summer, a fleet of four yachts sailed into the bay. Nobody in camp had ever seen anything like it. Two of the boats were each almost a hundred feet long, and the other two were only a few feet less grand.

The visitors stayed for a few days and were warm and friendly and got on famously with Mum and Dad. One yacht was owned by a family called Nordstum, or something like that. They said they owned a few department stores back home. Whatever.

The Americans we really got to know well were Don and Marlene Hudson, a glamorous couple from California. They spent every summer on their yacht, *The Genie,* and never failed to drop anchor in Orford Bay and stay a few days. Mum and Dad always invited them for dinner at our house, and they reciprocated by inviting my parents onboard *The Genie* for drinks, never a meal, because Marlene didn't know how to cook much besides canned soup and toast, and never both at the same time. My parents didn't mind. For them *The Genie* was a "porthole" to another world where everything was shipshape, from the teak decks to the gleaming brass railings, and Don and Marlene talked like movie stars, calling each other "Dahling" and throwing around adjectives like "fabulous" and "marvellous," as if those were normal words. Don served cocktails on a tray, and Marlene passed around celery sticks stuffed with Cheez Whiz and little hot dogs she called "cocktail sausages." It was the friggin' lap of luxury.

Marlene was Don's second wife, and she devoted herself to making his life perfect. Dad said she tried so hard because she was worried that Don might go for a "hat trick," whatever that was. She was always smiling and ready to hop to it if Don was disturbed, perturbed, or just bored. Her response to anything he proposed was, "Won't that be fun!" as if somebody pressed a button on the back of her neck and that exclamation popped out. I imagined Don saying, "Marlene, why don't you swim to Vancouver and get me that new fishing rod I've been thinking about?" and she would smile and say, "Won't that be fun!" before diving off the top deck of *The Genie* and breaststroking her way south.

One summer night when the Hudsons were at our house for dinner, Mum served the standard fare of oysters to start, a salmon for the main course, and blackberry pie for dessert. No big deal. This was food we got outside our front door—and it was free, not like those pricey cocktail sausages. However, Don and Marlene oohed and aahed over each dish, and when Mum placed a basket of her homemade buns on the table, Don turned to Marlene and solemnly whispered, "Dahling, the buns," like he'd just seen Jesus. I thought it was strange anybody could get emotional over a few buns, but shortly after "the bun moment," Don announced how "grand" it would be to take Suzy and Wendy and me out on *The Genie* for a few days. As my sisters and I squealed with excitement, Don turned to Marlene for confirmation of his brilliant idea and she did not fail him. "Won't that be fun!" she said right on cue, and gave her husband a nice, tight-lipped smile.

The thing was, Marlene kept *The Genie* shipshape, just the way Don liked it, so she was always sweeping and polishing like a regular Cinderella. I suppose that after being at our house and seeing wet bathing suits hung above the woodstove and piles of muddy boots on the front porch, she wasn't too keen on having three messy girls onboard.

For our first morning on *The Genie*, Marlene greeted us wearing an apron that looked like it had just been just taken out of a Macy's bag (because I saw her take it out of a Macy's bag). She ushered us to our designated seats around a beautifully set table and said, "Y'all probably eat flapjacks every morning, huh? So, that's what I'm going to make. Won't that be fun!" My sisters and I politely nodded yes, not knowing what flapjacks were.

Marlene set to work. She poured, she measured, she sifted, she stirred, stirred some more, stared at what she had stirred, referred to her cookbook, stirred again. Making flapjacks was very complicated—maybe a French recipe, I thought. Suzy offered to help but Marlene declined, and over the next hour she struggled to produce the flapjacks that we came to understand was the American word for hotcakes. After she had cooked the flapjacks to a brick-like consistency, she took a pound of frozen butter and cut it up into little rectangles, restaurant style. Nice touch, but we were starving, and just as we thought it was time to eat, she began to juice oranges. When breakfast was finally served, we each got four small, hard hotcakes and enough orange juice to quench the thirst of a hamster.

Despite the starvation diet, my sisters and I were thoroughly enjoying ourselves. Wendy and I spent most of our time on deck exchanging enthusiastic waves with other yachters cruising by, while Suzy relaxed in a deck chair with her nose in a book. Motoring down Bute Inlet, Don and Marlene pointed out eagles and seals and snow-covered mountain peaks. I suppose they thought we would find these things interesting, but it was all rather ordinary for three girls who had grown up surrounded by spectacular beauty. When Don spotted a pod of killer whales on the far side of the inlet, Wendy and I feigned interest while Suzy didn't even look up from her book. The Hudsons were unable to understand that we were having a great time just being on *The Genie*. Plus, we were on our way to Stuart Island, the social and economic hub of the coast, and that *was* guaranteed to be fun.

Of course, the best thing about Stuart Island was the general store. Previously, whenever our family visited the island, I had made a bee-line for the store, running up the dock and pushing through the heavy double doors into an entryway festooned with photos of movie stars such as Bing Crosby and John Wayne, proudly holding salmon they had caught. None of this impressed me. Fishing was the second-most boring thing on earth, something men did only when they got tired of doing the most boring thing on earth, which was golfing. I whizzed past the photos into the store and immediately got down to business, trolling the aisles for things I could buy with the twenty-five cents burning a hole in my pocket, and I was not disappointed. Mexican jumping beans and tubs of plasticine were priced just right.

However, this year was different. I was a year older and had two dollars, which I planned to spend like a drunken sailor on a movie magazine and a tube of pale pink lipstick. If there was any money left over, I might just blow it on a bottle of that cherry soda I saw kids on the dock guzzling to their hearts' content. After my shopping spree, I was going to sit in a deck chair on *The Genie*, basking in the glow of my newly-anointed lips while getting up to speed on Elizabeth Taylor's latest divorce. Don was right. Inviting us girls to spend a few days on *The Genie* was a grand idea.

But this was not meant to be. None of it. No pale pink lips, no Liz Taylor. Nada. All because Marlene decided that "Y'all are going fishing with one of those real nice Indian fellas. Won't that be fun!" What? Fishing? The second-most boring thing on earth? And before we knew it, the three of us were bobbing up and down in a speedboat in the middle of the Yuculta rapids. Suzy and Wendy sat on the middle bench listlessly holding their rods while I was in the bow with my rod stuck under the seat so I didn't even have to hold on to it. Our guide sat in the stern, handling the outboard motor and looking bored and depressed. I couldn't blame him. He knew we were not going to catch any fish, and I knew he wasn't going to get a tip—I hadn't saved two bucks to waste on a dumb fishing trip. As the hours dragged by, it became clear that Marlene had bought the "Deluxe All-Day Fishing Package."

Late that afternoon when we got back to *The Genie*, I think Marlene was feeling guilty because she announced that she was going to make milkshakes. What crazy American magic was this? There had never been a milkshake within a hundred miles of Stuart Island, and here was Marlene, of all people, making culinary history. I was confident she could pull this off because making milkshakes did not require any heat or stirring, and before long the optimistic sounds of ice crashing around in a blender could be heard from where we waited on the upper deck. And waited. And waited. Finally, Wendy went to investigate and shortly thereafter she appeared at the top of the steps proudly carrying a tray of frosty chocolate milkshakes. But that last step, the one with the raised sill on it, tripped her up and the milkshakes slid off the tray like the Ganges overflowing its banks in monsoon season, and a chocolaty sludge advanced across the deck

Within seconds, Marlene appeared with a bucket of water in one hand and a mop in the other, and she set to swabbing the deck as if her life depended on it. In the end, most of it came off. There were just a few spots that needed to be sanded—a point she mentioned about a thousand times.

By the time we got back to camp the next day, the Hudsons didn't seem sad to see us go. Don was kind enough to say that we should do it all again the following summer, but Marlene remained silent. She didn't say, "Won't that be fun!"

Things I Can Buy With $20

MY SISTERS AND I WERE NOT BATHING BEAUTIES AND IT ALL HAD to do with our swimsuits. Wendy's was too small. Dotty had given it to her, and I think it's fair to say that even though Wendy was only twelve, she was bigger than Dotty by a long shot, so the bathing suit was a little "snug." But that wasn't the worst of it. The suit had row upon row of ruffles, and I thought it made Wendy look like a toilet brush, though I didn't say as much. Suzy's suit was worse, a hand-me-down from Aunty Patty. Everybody knew she bought her bathing suits from the Salvation Army, so there was a pretty good chance that the faded blue swimsuit was from a dead lady and that the dead lady had drowned in her faded blue suit.

My suit was the most *au courant,* a lovely pale-yellow number, but I had gotten black oil all over the front of it from rolling oil drums to the cookhouse, one of my summer jobs until Franky and Wendy fired me for being "too careful." My other job was making beds in the bunkhouse. I had been guaranteed a salary of twenty dollars for the summer and in anticipation of payday, I was compiling a list of things I planned to buy, creatively titled: "Things I Can Buy With $20." Each item on the list was a piece of clothing, including white go-go boots, a miniskirt, and, most importantly, a real bikini with spaghetti straps, just like the ones in *Seventeen* magazine. My sisters were also crazy about clothes, and we spent hours perusing a variety of magazines, circling items we liked. But if you had lined the three of us up in our bathing suits, it would have appeared that clothes were the last thing on our minds—a situation we made no effort to change since there was no one of importance in Orford Bay we needed to impress.

However, that all changed early one July morning. I awoke to see that another American yacht had slipped into the bay during the night and tied up to our float. Peering through binoculars, I spotted three teenage girls, typical Americans: tall, slim, blond, and tanned—at least, that's how I thought all teens from the U.S. looked, thanks, again, to *Seventeen* magazine. I hoped the girls would want to become friends with my sisters and me. We could each have our own pen pal, and after years of heart-to-heart letter writing we would be bridesmaids for each other. Hopefully, Wendy's dress would not have ruffles like her bathing suit.

Abruptly coming back to my senses, I saw movement on the yacht. One of the girls had disembarked to stick a toe into the frosty waters of Orford Bay only to yank it out with lightning speed. "This water is rahlly cold!" she shouted up to her friends on deck. "The water in California is soooo much betterrrr." I was torn, not knowing how to react. She had insulted our bay but had done so with such a glorious drawl, I wanted to hear more complaints. Luckily, she obliged. "I rahlly wanna go swimmiiiing," she moaned, "but I might catch pneumoniaaaa!" As the last vowel drifted across the water, I realized that this girl was the most sophisticated person I had ever laid eyes on.

When Dad came home from work that day, he reported that the yacht had engine trouble and wasn't going anywhere until a mechanic flew into camp to do some repairs. Manna from Heaven! The girls were stuck in Orford Bay! For the next twenty-four hours, Suzy and Wendy joined me at the kitchen window, and we listened to the girls say the most wonderful things like, "Gimmeeee the suntan lotion willyaaaa," and my sisters and I repeated "willyaaaa" like parrots on Xanax. In no time at all, we were completely fluent in Californian, saying things like "soooo graaate," and "rahlly niiiice," until Mum put her foot down, insisting that Americans did not, and never would, speak the Queen's

English as we did. And if we kept acting like Americans, we'd grow up unable to find Canada on a map of North America and never stop boasting about how the United States single-handedly won WWII. Of course, Wendy had to remind Mum that we actually didn't speak like the Queen, but Mum insisted that we spoke "Canadian" Queen's English, which was exactly the same as the real thing, except with a different accent.

Mum also strongly recommended that we put down the binoculars, leave our post at the kitchen window, and invite the girls to go swimming at our lake, which was about an hour's walk up the mountain along the logging road. That was a great idea! It was obvious that their delicate constitutions could not bear the chilly waters of Orford Bay. The lake was much warmer—well, less marrow-sucking cold than the bay. So Wendy and I rowed out to the yacht, introduced ourselves, and, without too much persuading, the girls agreed to do my sisters and me the giant favour of letting us try to entertain them for a day. But what, for the love of God, were we going to wear? Besides learning a new language over the past few days, we had also been keen observers of the never-ending fashion show onboard the yacht. The girls appeared on deck every few hours in different outfits and each item of clothing looked clean, pressed, and, I suspected, not from the Salvation Army.

The only solution was to wear our "ferry clothes," the special matching outfits that Mum made every year for our migration up the coast. These clothes were nearly as important as Christmas dresses and church coats, but they had a homespun look, making us appear as if we'd recently escaped from a religious cult and were trying, but failing, to integrate back into mainstream society. Plus, this year's outfits were particularly bad: slacks and thick wool sweaters in mauve, a colour Suzy called "old cheese." But they were the best clothes we had, and Mum gave us the okay to wear them—just this once.

As luck would have it, the next day was a scorcher and trudging to the lake in itchy sweaters and long pants soon became unbearable, though our guests seemed to be suffering more than me and my sisters as they plodded along in shorts and t-shirts, complaining loudly about the mosquitoes, the dust, the heat, and repeatedly asking, "How much furrrrrthurrrr?" I didn't mention how lucky we were that it was a Sunday, the loggers' day off, so there were no trucks whizzing past every five minutes forcing us off the road. Instead, I tried to take their minds off their unbearably painful circumstances by asking them about life in California. Their answers were monosyllabic and sarcastic, and I admired the way they were naturally bitchy, exactly the type of teenager I wanted to be.

By the time we reached the lake, everyone was ready for a swim, and that's when the Yanks unveiled their very best fashion statements. Under their shirts and shorts they were wearing bikinis, exactly the kind I wanted, and right then and there I knew I didn't want to go swimming. I sensed Suzy and Wendy felt the same, but it was so damn hot we had to swallow our collective pride and strip down to our swimwear: "toilet brush suit," "drowned lady's suit," "oil slick suit." Suzy was so embarrassed she blurted out that she had ordered a new bathing suit from Eaton's catalogue but it hadn't arrived yet. The girls responded with "uh huhhhh" and rolled their eyes at each other. I felt my sister's burning shame, though I tried not to be angry and still held onto hope for a pact of international sisterhood.

They didn't like swimming in the lake. It was slimy and had too many living things in it. Apparently in California they didn't have lakes, just swimming pools, and chlorine killed anything that wriggled.

Next up was a tour round the lake in a rowboat that leaked like a sieve. The six of us piled in. Wendy rowed and I bailed like mad with a rusty coffee can while Suzy acted as tour director, pointing out beaver houses, loons, and eagle nests. The Yanks didn't show much interest; they were busy talking to each other about previous vacations they had shared, like the time they flew over an active volcano in Hawaii, went up the "I Fell Tower" in Paris, which sounded a little dangerous if you asked me, and shopped in New York, blah, blah, blah, all of which was an attempt to make Suzy and Wendy and me feel bad. By the time we got back to camp, I had changed my mind about the girls and that night I crossed "bikini" off my "Things I Can Buy With $20" list.

Chapter Seven
Pass the Spuds

The confidence of grizzly bears, why men don't eat salad, and how Franky defeated a Nazi.

Hotcakes

CAMP COOKS WERE LIKE HOCKEY GOALIES, INDISPENSABLE TO the team but separate from the other players. Cooks worked alone and lived alone, and they liked it that way. In Orford Bay, the cook had a bedroom at the back of the cookhouse that resembled a monk's cell in its simplicity. There was a single bed in the corner and an (empty) dynamite box for a bedside table and that was about it, except for the bottles of booze under the bed. Many camp cooks drank, and our cook Dave was no exception, yet he managed to turn out delicious meals day in, day out while working in a kitchen that had no electricity or refrigeration. He cooked by the light of kerosene lamps and stored perishables in a pantry at the back of the cookhouse where cool air blowing in through a screen door usually kept the food fresh enough to eat. Of course, he always bolted the door so raccoons and other vermin couldn't get in, but he wasn't told that a screen door is really just gossamer to a bear. Nobody wanted to upset the cook.

Every morning, Dave rolled out of bed at 4:30 am, lit an oil lamp, lit a cigarette, threw an apron overtop his flannel shirt and jeans, and was officially ready to begin work. His first task was to get the oil stove roaring hot so breakfast could be served the moment the loggers sat down in the dining hall at 6:00 am. Hotcakes were the staple breakfast food, and Dave churned out stacks of them each morning while keeping an eye on frying pans sizzling with bacon and eggs, a lineup of coffee pots perking on the back of the stove, and toast browning in the oven. Then, with the grace of a ballerina, albeit one hungover and wearing bedroom slippers, he carried platter after platter of food into the dining hall, piping hot and piled high, and it just kept on coming until the last drops of syrup were sopped up with bits of toast and the men pushed their plates away without so much as a thank you.

After breakfast, each logger made his own lunch from a mountain of food Dave had laid out on a sideboard. There was homemade bread, cut thick for big sandwiches, and a selection of fillings to satisfy almost any taste: sliced ham, chicken, beef, fresh-caught salmon, cheddar cheese, egg salad, you name it. Next came the pies; apple, cherry, peach, raisin, take your pick. Then brownies, matrimonial cake, Nanaimo bars, chocolate layer cake, and homemade cookies. Everything got wrapped up in wax paper and piled into lunch buckets along with thermoses of coffee laced with Carnation Evaporated Milk, poured thick and sweet from the can.

Each logger had his first name painted on the front of his lunch bucket so there were no mix-ups. Ernie, Andy, Harry, Floyd, and Mike were the core group of the crew. They had worked together for years, and their lunch buckets were dented and scraped and smelled like coffee and bread and hard work. A shiny new lunch bucket indicated that a logger was a rookie, the worst ones being the university students who only worked in camp for the summer. They ate peanut butter sandwiches and never shut the hell up. Sometimes, one of these know-it-alls opened their lunch bucket at midday to find it full of rocks, but nobody knew how that happened.

When the loggers left for work, Dave got a move on, baking while the ovens were still hot. After that, he began prepping for dinner, peeling a wheelbarrow's worth of potatoes and carrots, selecting a slab of meat from the pantry, and making up individual dishes of celery, tomatoes, and radishes that were served in lieu of salad because, as Mum always said, "Salad is too complicated for men." At precisely 5:00 pm, Dave rang the dinner bell. It was the same routine as breakfast, just different food and in quantities that could have satisfied Paul Bunyan. Afterwards, the men returned to the bunkhouse, stuffed to the gills, and rested up for a few hours before returning to the cookhouse once more, this time for coffee and dessert just so nobody went to bed hungry.

The margin for error in the cookhouse was slim. Loggers worked hard and when they came back to camp at the end of the day there wasn't a lot to do besides eat and go to bed, so meals had to be delicious, varied, and enormous. If a logger didn't like something about a meal, he'd never address the cook directly. Instead, the guy with the gripe would say something like "I need a goddamned axe to cut this meat" loud enough that the cook could hear the complaint in the kitchen. If an entire crew became disgruntled about the grub, the cook was fired, which meant Mum and Aunty Patty had to fill in until a new cook was hired. They didn't like that much because, even between the two of them, the job was damn hard work.

The good thing about Mum and Aunty Patty cooking for the loggers was that my sisters and I and Franky got to eat in the cookhouse. This was exciting, not because of the riveting dinner table conversation, as there wasn't any, but because it was a chance to spend time with the loggers. When dinnertime rolled around, the crew arrived in the cookhouse showered, shaved, and smelling of Lifebuoy soap. Each man sat in his regular spot and began eating right away. There was no preamble, no prayers, no small talk, no jokes. The ex-cons never made eye contact with anyone and sat hunched over the table with one arm firmly wrapped around their plates. Uncle Floyd said it was because they were used to guys in jail taking their food or knocking their plates onto the floor. The only words spoken were requests like: "pass the spuds," "gimme the salt," or for a real enlightening moment, we might hear: "I think it's gonna rain tomorrow." But Dad had told us stories about what went on up the hill so we felt we knew each of the loggers quite well.

One blatant breach of etiquette I never attempted was to hold my cutlery the way most of the loggers did: thumbs up, forks and knives pointing down. I knew my days in the cookhouse were numbered, and I'd soon be back at home where more ladylike behavior was required.

The routine in the cookhouse never varied, though cooks came and went. Some were bad cooks, some were bad drunks, and some were both, but Dave was the best cook of all because he was a happy drunk and could cook like nobody's business. His only concern was that he might be on the menu if a bear dropped by the cookhouse for a bite to eat, even though Dad and Uncle Kurt repeatedly reassured him he had nothing to worry about. They told him bears rarely came into camp, especially grizzlies; they were much too timid.

Nevertheless, the XL-sized grizzly Dave came face to face with early one morning in the cookhouse proved, beyond doubt, that there are exceptions to every rule. Moreover, the bear was quite confident, walking straight through the latched screen door, devouring the contents of the meat cooler, then sauntering back into the woods.

Dave left camp shortly after the raid on the cooler. He said he couldn't stop worrying about bears, even the ones with poor self-confidence. Everyone was sorry to see him go, and Uncle Kurt said he hoped the next cook would be a lot like Dave, "somebody who cooks real good and is never too hungover to get out of bed in the morning."

Hasenpfeffer and Spanferkel

AFTER DAVE QUIT, MUM AND AUNTY PATTY WERE LEFT TO PICK
up the slack in the cookhouse and, to be honest, they were not the
greatest camp cooks. The only experience they had preparing food
for large groups came from church picnics and Girl Guide cookouts,
so they occasionally missed the mark when cooking for loggers. Like
the time Aunty Patty served a dinner of potato salad and cold salmon,
violating the first commandment of cookhouse dinners, which states
that all food must be served hot otherwise it would be called "lunch,"
and what, for the love of Christ, had she been thinking? Another time,
Mum put a tablecloth on the dining table, "to make it nice," but when
the crew entered the cookhouse there ensued a brief discussion among
the more talkative of the group about why there was a bedsheet on the
table. Thankfully, not long after the "cold food/love-of-Christ meal"
and the "tablecloth incident," a letter arrived in camp from a woman
named Louisa inquiring about the position of camp cook. I don't know
who was more relieved, the loggers or Mum and Aunty Patty.

Louisa wrote that she had experience cooking for hungry soldiers and that her specialties included dishes called *Hasenpfeffer* and
Spanferkel, which Dad said he hoped was not Chinese food because
"the guys are not gonna go for that," but she got the job anyhow.

When her plane landed, Franky and I ran down to the float to greet her. First, the door of the Beaver swung open and a substantial suitcase was heaved into the arms of the pilot who was standing on the float. He took hold of it and almost collapsed, unaware it was full of cast-iron frying pans. Then Louisa appeared. She too was substantial and proceeded cautiously down the steps of the plane, leaning heavily on the pilot who really looked like he was done for this time but, somehow, managed to bear the burden. After that, Louisa wobbled her way up to the cookhouse followed by Franky and me dragging the suitcase. Later, we concluded that Louisa probably weighed about three-and-a-half suitcases full of frying pans.

I thought our new cook's girth might be a good indication of her culinary expertise but I was only half right. Louisa did turn out to be a great cook. However, the reason she was so fat, she informed Franky and me, was not that she ate too much but because calories seeped into her fingertips when she was cooking. Apparently, she only had to put her hands into a bowl of dough or handle a rib roast and she instantly gained a few pounds. What could she do about it? Just get fat, that's what. I figured she was an oddball, but harmless nonetheless, never imagining that some of her beliefs were deeply disturbing, if not horrifying.

The war had been over for almost twenty years, but she had remained loyal to "der Führer," and every chance she got, she droned on about him as if he were her adorable younger brother who some people just didn't "get." For the first few weeks, everybody overlooked her love of Adolf because she seemed only slightly deranged and the crew loved her cooking.

When she wasn't absorbing calories through her fingertips, Louisa often joined Wendy, Franky, and me swimming off the float, and she'd reminisce about the "good old days" in Germany when Hitler first came to power. Apparently, there were lots of jobs and food, and the whole country was just a fun place to be. Also, she never failed to remind us about how tepid the water in Orford Bay was for her because as a teenager she had joined a club called "Hitlerjugend," and all the members really enjoyed swimming in freezing cold lakes in order to build up their strength and stamina. This reminded me of Auntie Lorna who boasted about how her kids loved liver and onions and going to church and math—all that stuff that was never fun, you were just forced to do it.

We never argued with her. After all, she was a great cook, and we knew not to upset her in case she quit. But one afternoon on the float, when she was going on about "der Führer," Wendy asked her about the Holocaust. We had read *The Diary of Anne Frank* that summer, and the story was fresh in our minds. Louisa scoffed, "Those people, they had too much. Something had to be done," and just like that, the temperature on the float plummeted. Wendy and I were left shivering in our wet bathing suits, not knowing what to say. Then Franky, who we thought hadn't been listening, piped up, "Hey Louisa, look at me! Look at me! Here's your dumb Führer for you!" and he began goose-stepping around the float, alternating the Nazi salute with armpit farts, the kind young boys excel at, all the while yelling, "Der Führer's a farter! Der Führer's a farter!" Now it was Louisa who didn't know what to say as Franky continued to goose-step the entire length of the stiff leg while shouting insults that remained within the theme of Hitler and farts.

Things got worse for our resident Nazi. Early one morning, a tag team of raccoons climbed through a window at the back of the cookhouse, and by the time she discovered the furry visitors, three trays of her pastries had been devoured, which also proved how great they were since the raccoons had so many other things to choose from, like whole chickens and dozens of eggs. And the really unfortunate thing was that Louisa didn't know you can't just shoo raccoons out of the way when they are busy eating fistfuls of *Gugelhupfen* nor did she understand that a raccoon will bite when you try to lift it up and up and throw it out of your kitchen. In the end, it was Louisa who ended up outside, yelling for help, while the raccoons stayed put, stuffing their faces.

Not long after that, she quit, flying into a rage and saying nobody respected her, which was true, and we didn't *like* her a whole hell of

Chapter Eight

The Truth About Loggers

Knife-sharpening lessons from a murderer, the curse of pointy-toe shoes,
and the significance of hooped skirts.

Come in, Bugaboo Bay

LOGGING CAMPS DID NOT HAVE MUCH TO OFFER IN THE WAY OF conventional forms of entertainment. The closest movie theatre was about a hundred miles away, and since we didn't have electricity, we couldn't play records or listen to the radio. Television was also out of the question, except for the time the loggers got hold of an old black-and-white TV, hooked it up to the camp's generator, and tried to watch the Stanley Cup playoffs. The reception was so bad it looked like the games were being played on an outdoor rink in blizzard conditions. One logger walked around camp with a set of rabbit ear antennae while guys in front of the television shouted instructions to him like, "No, no! Oh! Yeah! Okay. Don't move! I think we can see . . . Nahhhhhh!" Then one night a logger came running over to our house, burst through the front door, and yelled, "John, John, come quick! Come quick! We can see the puck!"

Other than these brief hockey highlights, there was another more reliable source of entertainment in camp, and that was our radio telephone. It allowed us to listen in on calls made to or from any logging camp on the coast. The calls were uncut, uncensored, and way more interesting than any dumb hockey game, puck or no puck.

The radio telephone was about the size of a beer fridge, and it sat on top of a desk in one corner of our kitchen. It had loads of knobs and dials that nobody knew what to do with except for the ones marked, *On, Off*, and *Volume*. There was also another unmarked dial that may or may not have had something to do with controlling the static on the line. Anybody making a call fiddled with this dial, just in case it worked, hoping that the person they called wouldn't sound as if they were having their hair cut with a power saw. Weekdays, the calls were quite boring, all about ordering machinery parts and repairs, that kind of thing, but come Saturday night, our family gathered round the radio telephone because that's when things got interesting. Loggers called home and received calls from loved ones. The conversations were always entertaining, and sometimes alarming.

Every call was routed through Vancouver, and it was fun to listen to the operators call camps with names like Whaletown, Squirrel Cove, or our favourite, Bugaboo Bay. Hearing that name repeated over and over was like poetry: "This is the Vancouver operator calling Bugaboo Bay. Come in Bugaboo Bay." After a few minutes, if there was no answer, the operator would continue with "Vancouver calling Bugaboo Bay. Are you answering? Come in, Bugaboo Bay." Another pause, some crackling on the line, and then a voice, loud and strong, "Vancouver, this is Bugaboo Bay, over." Our kitchen erupted in cheers because we knew Bugaboo Bay was just a tiny camp with about three loggers, and when they got a call, it was cause for celebration.

When an operator called our camp, Mum or Dad would pick up, find out who the call was for, and tell the operator to stand by, while I was dispatched to the bunkhouse, running at top speed to inform the logger who was getting the call that he better put on some pants and get over to our house without delay. Most of the time, our family stayed in the kitchen and listened to the calls, but at other times, if the conversation got too lovey-dovey or volatile, my sisters and I were sent outside.

When a logger called his wife, he sat down at the telephone desk, picked up the handheld microphone, and said, "Vancouver, this is Orford Bay. Come in." After that, he'd sit back, light up a smoke, and chat with Mum and Dad while he waited for the operator to call back, so he could give her his wife's telephone number. Then, he waited a few more minutes while the operator dialed the number, got the wife on the line, and asked, "Madam, will you accept a call from Orford Bay?" Sometimes a woman refused to take a call, and the logger sitting in our kitchen would shout down the line something like, "Come on, Judith! Fer Chrissakes, take the goddamned call!" Outbursts like this always elicited firm reprimands from the operators, who would say, "Sir, I am going to have to ask you to refrain from using foul language. If this happens again, I will terminate the call." And she meant it.

Women often called their husbands to ask for money to pay the rent or buy groceries, and if they had been drinking and were making no sense whatsoever, the operator would cut into the call and say, "Madam, have you had a drink tonight? Perhaps you would like to call back another time?" Then she'd cut the call. Mum reassured me and my sisters that if Mrs. Johansen (it was always her) hadn't been drinking and smoking so much, she could have paid the rent and bought some food. How my mother could hear Mrs. Johansen smoking over the static on the line, I had no idea, but I knew she could see around corners and read minds, so supersonic hearing was probably not much of a stretch for her.

Occasionally, we'd hear a call from the RCMP wanting information regarding the whereabouts of a certain individual. One time, the police were looking for Mr. Kenneth R. Lalond who had worked in Orford Bay a few years earlier. When Dad heard this, he remarked, "Oh, they want to talk to Kenny, eh? I heard he stabbed a guy in a bar in Campbell River. 'Course, Uncle Kurt and I had to fire him. Bit of a short fuse." When I heard that, I was stunned. Kenny was one of the few loggers who had always been willing to play baseball with us. Sure, he got a little testy if he struck out, but other than that he was a great guy and taught us kids how to sharpen our jackknives by spitting on a sharpening stone and grinding the blades until they were razor sharp.

Other calls from family members were equally hair-raising, like the time Dad's cousin, Bubbles, called to ask if the camp needed a cook. She said she wanted to work because she was lonely since her boys had left home. Dad asked her where they had gone, and she replied,

"Oh, not far. They're just down the road at the penitentiary. I visit them all the time, but it's just not the same as having them here, you know what I mean?" She went on to explain that the "boys" were in jail for armed robbery, "but they didn't mean any harm. The shotguns weren't even loaded." My father told Bubbles that he hoped the boys would get parole soon, but, unfortunately, he had just hired a cook.

On nights like this, I went to bed wondering about life's big questions: Was Mrs. Johansen drinking because she was poor? Did Kenny mean to stab the guy in the bar, or was his knife just too damn sharp? And were you guilty of armed robbery if your shotgun wasn't loaded?

LOGGERS' SPORTS

MOST YEARS, OUR FAMILY ARRIVED BACK IN VANCOUVER IN
time to attend the Pacific National Exhibition, or P.N.E., with its standard midway attractions, including stomach-churning rides, artery-
clogging food, and a loggers' sports show we never missed. It was fun
to watch burly guys throw axes, log roll, and race up poles like their
pants were on fire. But unlike any loggers I had ever seen, these loggers never stopped smiling and they wore clean clothes and new boots.
What was this? Happy, clean loggers? I was used to seeing men arrive
back in camp at the end of each day exhausted and caked in mud so
thick they sometimes threw themselves into the saltchuck just to get
the worst of it off. Besides, I knew what real loggers' sports were.

First and foremost, every logger in Orford Bay was a champion
napper. After work, as soon as they were showered and changed, they
dove for their beds, pointed their toes skyward, and snoozed until the
dinner bell rang. On Sundays, their one day off, the naps were not just
short sprints but real marathons. We kids were not supposed to go near
the bunkhouse in case we woke the men, but of course Franky forgot,
ricocheting back and forth past the bunkhouse until one of the men
stuck his head out the door and yelled, "Jesus H. Christ! Stop running
or I'll wring your neck!" Franky would screech to a halt, walk slowly
for about a dozen paces, then take off again, full speed.

Another sporting event the loggers enjoyed was chin-ups. They'd stand around smoking and taking turns on a bar, a few of the guys even doing one-handed pull-ups, but soon everyone got bored and wandered back to the bunkhouse to nap some more.

For indoor sports, there was the tool shed. It was an old floathouse, positioned about four feet off the ground on a platform of logs, same as all the other camp buildings, but it was open on the front like a carport, and the interior walls and ceiling had been removed. This was where any piece of machinery diagnosed as "haywire" was either repaired or abandoned, as evidenced by the engine parts scattered across the floor, up the walls, and hanging from the rafters. Everything was slick with oil and grease, and stepping inside the shed was like walking into an over-turned jar of molasses. My sisters and I avoided the place, not because of the grime, but because there were holes in the floor big enough to swallow any one of us into the swill of oil and sewage beneath the shed.

The holes were a result of what I called "Loggers' Sports Day," except there was only one event. Men showed up in the tool shed to prove their worth by doing something that only men are willing to do (because women think stuff like this is stupid) and that was to lift a 150 pound anvil over their heads. Though I have to admit most of the contestants had some finesse: they lifted the anvil with a smooth "clean and jerk," then staggered around a bit while swearing through clenched teeth before dropping the unwieldy burden—right through the floor.

After about a half-dozen anvils disappeared under the shed, Dad declared anvil-lifting no longer a legitimate sport in Orford Bay. He suggested that horseshoes were a good alternative because they were cheaper than anvils and could only knock a guy's teeth out, whereas an anvil could do a lot more damage and keep a logger off work.

The only "real" loggers' sport in camp was log rolling, though it was a little different from what we saw at the P.N.E. There, two men stood on a small log in a kid-size swimming pool, rolling a log backwards and forwards, going slow and then fast, until one opponent lost his balance and fell into the water. Game over.

When the sport was introduced in Orford Bay, the loggers took to it like ducks to water—literally. Dad cut the end off a log that was about five feet in diameter and ten feet long, and this was the official log for rolling. It was actually meant for us kids but some of the loggers just couldn't help showing off, stepping onto the log fully clothed, boots on, cigarette in hand—which was Wendy's cue to show up. She never outright challenged any of the men; they just thought they'd humour her. After all, how could this young girl possibly roll a log better than they could? What they didn't know was that during the day, while they were at work, my sister ran around that log like a hamster on a wheel.

Typically, an unsuspecting logger would hop onto the log with Wendy and as it got going faster and faster, the cigarette would be cast aside with a quick sizzle as it hit the water, and a few seconds later the logger would hit the water, too, coming to the surface spluttering in disbelief. Pulling himself onto the float, he'd check to see if his wristwatch was still working (it wasn't), then he'd squelch his way back to the bunkhouse, put his boots by the woodstove to dry overnight (they didn't), and after that, he'd take a nap because that's what loggers did best.

Log rolling with Wendy.

They're in my Pants!

BESIDES CRAZY COOKS, THERE WAS ALWAYS SOME FORM OF WILD-
life creating havoc in Orford Bay, and it usually wasn't the bears. They
were forthright animals and did not shit on toothbrushes or hide in
cupboards like the small creatures that showed up in camp each spring
and made themselves right at home.

Snakes were the worst of the lot. The garter snake season began with
"mating balls," which sound like a kind of sex toy but are actually no fun
at all unless you are a snake. Late one afternoon, as Wendy, Franky, and I
were walking along a narrow path that, well, snaked through the woods
behind camp, we came upon a tall stump moving and throbbing with a
life force all its own, a mating ball. We stopped dead. Snakes were pouring out of the hollow stump by the dozens, twisting and coiling round
each other, then dropping to the ground near our feet where they continued to contort as if they'd landed on a hot stove. We stood transfixed,
not daring to move, and unable to take our eyes off what was happening
in front of us until Wendy got up the courage to grab my hand, and I
grabbed Franky's, and we sidestepped past the mass of wriggling rep-
tiles. Once free, we ran like hell all the way home and, in the safety of our
kitchen, Franky reported to Mum that he hadn't been scared in the least,
though he was as wild-eyed as Wendy and I.

By the end of summer, encounters with snakes became less dra-
matic and just part of everyday life. In the outhouse, they coiled up in

the corners watching us with dead-eyed stares as we went about our business. But they could be friendly as well, going so far as to keep Aunty Patty company one afternoon as she dozed off while suntanning on the beach. A fat garter snake joined her, eschewing the rocky beach for her smooth abdomen. When Suzy walked by and spotted the two sunbathers, she wasn't sure what to do: wake Aunty Patty and let all hell break loose, or just hope the snake would shove off before she woke up? Suzy chose the latter solution, and our dear aunt never figured out why she had a stripe of white skin across her tanned belly.

Unlike snakes, the field mice we had one summer were adorable. Their big brown eyes and huge ears reminded me of the mice in Disney's *Cinderella*, except these ones didn't sing. At first, there were just one or two bouncing across the kitchen floor, nothing to worry about at all. It was fun to toss bits of food their way and marvel at how fast they could scarf it down before scuttling under the couch. Darling, absolutely darling.

But in less than twenty-four hours, the rodents seemed to have multiplied a thousandfold, and in no time at all they had taken over the camp, chewing into every bag of flour and sugar, prying lids off jars, and unscrewing bottle tops with mousy dexterity. Nothing was unappetizing to the palate of these terrestrial piranhas. They ate the leather shoelaces off caulk boots, drank stale beer, and nibbled on sticks of dynamite. The cookhouse was hit the hardest. Every case of food was gnawed through and littered with mice poop.

In the midst of the invasion, Mum opened a cake tin one afternoon and came face to face with a mouse caught chocolate-handed, stuffing globs of icing into its already-bulging cheeks. Shrieking, she tossed the tin into the air, and we watched, mesmerized, as the robust rodent performed an airshow of loop-de-loops and spins before planting a perfect four-point landing and buggering off. The dumb ones were not so lucky. They drowned in thermoses of coffee and did the dead-mouse float in pots of soup.

In the bunkhouse, loggers found that their tobacco pouches, wallets, and other appetizing leather tidbits had been nibbled on and then shat all over for good measure. We would hear boots stomping, a door thrown open, then the assaulted item would go sailing through the air. Franky and I thought these outbursts were fantastic and re-enacted the highly emotive scenes to see who could act the most outraged. But as usual, it was Dotty who stole the show when she upended a ketchup bottle overtop a burger and a dead mouse fell out, "plop," right onto the bun. She stared at the mouse in horror before her eyes rolled back in her head and she slid off her chair, pulling the tablecloth along with her in a cascade of dishes and ketchupy mouse burger. It was one of her best performances.

Then one morning around 5:00, Suzy, Wendy, and I were woken by Dad yelling, "They're in my pants! They're in my pants!" We jumped out of bed and ran into the kitchen to witness our father twirling round Cossack-style, slapping his legs and madly shaking one booted foot in the air, then the other. There were mice in his pants, but to the north everything was zipped up and buttoned, and to the south his caulk boots were blocking the exits. Mum chased him around the kitchen lunging at him with a pair of scissors. If she could cut the suspenders, his pants would fall down and the mice could escape.

To make matters worse, all the crashing and yelling woke every field mouse that had been enjoying our accommodations. They rushed into the fray, hopping up and down like they were on mouse trampolines. Our kitchen was swarming with mice, and our father had snapped. He was crushing every mouse within stomping range while Mum screamed, "Noooooooo!" But it was too late. It was a mouse massacre.

When the melee was over, my sisters and I looked at the squished mice, looked at our maniacal parents, one with his pants around his ankles, the other in her nightgown, clutching a pair of scissors, and we went back to bed, convinced that our parents truly were deranged—just as we had always suspected.

Idol Threats

THE POUNDING BEGAN JUST AS HE WAS DOZING OFF. "BAM! Bam! Bam!" It was a Sunday afternoon in August, and most of the guys, like Ernie, were lying on their beds, smoking, reading month-old newspapers, or snoozing. They were resting up for another week of fire season hours, starting work at 5:00 every morning to avoid the heat of the day, when hot-running engines sparked fires. "Bam!" There it was again, smashing into the outside wall of the bunkhouse right above Ernie's bed, and he noticed the butts in his ashtray had jiggled over to one side, piling up on top of each other. Nobody moved. It was hot in the bunkhouse, and the men lacked the energy to get up and see what the racket was all about. Besides, the intervals between the strikes were growing longer as if the perpetrator was also losing his vitality. Ernie rolled over and closed his eyes, resting in the silence for a few precious minutes before the pounding started up again. "Bam! Bam! Bam!"

"That's it!" he announced, getting up and heading for the door. "I'm gonna kill that sonofabitch."

The guys in the bunkhouse watched him go. They knew Ernie wouldn't tolerate any BS, like the way he stopped the new guy, Steve, from reading the Bible, not that there was anything wrong with that, it was just that he wanted to read the Bible aloud, at night, when they were tired. Steve said he wanted to "save" them, and no loud protests or cigarette butts flicked in his direction could shut him up until Ernie ripped the good book out of his hands, saying, "Now, you know who's saved, Steve? You're saved because I didn't punch you in the head." He handed the Bible back, cautioning Steve to "keep that stuff to yourself."

Now, coming around the back of the bunkhouse, Ernie expected to see one of the guys with a bat and ball, or, well, he wasn't exactly sure what, but he had definitely not anticipated seeing Franky gripping the handle of a very large axe. And before Ernie could stop him, the kid lifted it over his head, took a step forward and let go, slamming the blade deep into the side of the bunkhouse. "Bam!"

Ernie was taken aback, but he wasted no time contemplating the unpredictability of life. Wrenching the axe out of the wall, he turned on Franky, "Do you want me to cut your hands off? Maybe a leg? Because, if you do, I'll do it for you real quick," and he marched off the way he had come, but stopped and turned back to warn Franky: "If you ever pick one of these up again, I'll wring your neck."

To be fair, most of the loggers were big on threatening to wring Franky's neck, especially when he ran past the bunkhouse doing his Tarzan yell while they were trying to sleep. But as he watched Ernie disappear around the corner of the bunkhouse, Franky got the feeling Ernie was not the kind of guy who made idle threats.

Ernie had been hired in July when the weather was perfect: no rain and no fires. The truckers were hauling logs ten hours a day, six days a week. Then Harry, one of the drivers, "decides to bust his appendix," Uncle Kurt complained to Dad. "We gotta get a guy in here real quick, but it's gonna be tough gettin' a good one. I guess I'll try the agency."

The Logger's Employment Agency, located on East Hastings Street, was the place where Uncle Kurt and Dad had lined up for jobs when they were fifteen years old, two skinny teenagers, willing to take anything they were offered. But that was a long time ago, and these days Uncle Kurt wondered aloud if "those guys at the agency just walk across the street to the beer parlour and shout, 'Is anybody in here lookin' for work? You gotta be able to drive a truck or sumpin' like that.' And that's why we get all them duds."

He had a point. It was hard to get good workers, especially in the summer months when all the camps were working flat out. The last guy the agency sent showed up wearing sunglasses and pointy-toe shoes, a far cry from the loggers who arrived in camp ready to work, boots on, hard hat in hand.

From our kitchen window, Wendy and I had watched the new guy climb out of the Beaver, well aware his flagrant disregard for proper logger attire was going to get him fired on the spot. "Ohhhhhh, Dad is not gonna like that," Wendy reported, peering through the binoculars. "Oh, get a load of those sunglasses, and I think he's got . . . wait a sec, yeah, he's got one of those rat-tailed combs in his back pocket. Here, you take a look," she said, handing me the binoculars. "Can you see it? It's white, just like a girl's. Dad is definitely not gonna like that."

Ernie arrived in Orford Bay carrying his belongings in a paper bag and wearing cowboy boots that made his walk along the stiff leg extremely entertaining for my sister and me. "Come here!" Wendy called from the kitchen. "Look at this guy! He almost fell in!" And for the next few minutes we traded the binoculars back and forth, fully appreciating his distress until I shouted: "Here he comes!" and we dropped onto the floor, giggling, as Ernie walked up to the house and knocked on the door.

He'd come to ask Mum for an advance on his first paycheque for the work pants and suspenders and other things he needed from the commissary. She told him caulk boots had to be ordered from Dayton's and wouldn't arrive for a month so he'd have to make do with an old pair of Dad's, and she went to get them off the back porch. Afterwards, when she asked him to fill out an income tax form, he pulled his ID out of a hand-tooled leather wallet, and she recognized it as a handicraft guys learned in jail.

On his first day on the job, Ernie joined the convoy of trucks heading up the mountain. It was still dark, and the tight turns and ruts got him worrying about coming back down with a load of logs. But pulling into the loading area, there was no more time to think. The logs were loaded onto the truck in a flash, well past the stanchions and not chained down, and seconds later he found himself racing down the mountain, keeping up with the guy in front of him, and conscious of the guy on his tail. He dropped his first load over the dump at 6:00 am and took off back up the mountain. By quitting time, Uncle Kurt remarked that Ernie was "gonna work out real good."

⁓\ı/⁓

ON HOT DAYS, ALL OF US KIDS WENT SWIMMING AT OUR LAKE. It took about an hour to get there, depending on the number of times we had to run for cover upon hearing the rumble of an approaching truck. "Get off the road!" we yelled to each other and scrambled for high ground to avoid any stray logs tumbling off the truck.

Arriving at the lake, we made our way through thickets of huckleberry to reach the water's edge, stripped down to bathing suits, and dove in. Franky and Wendy challenged each other to race to the far-off beaver dam, while Suzy took up position on a log and read the afternoon away. I paddled between the submerged snags, clutching slimy branches whenever I needed to catch my breath. I swear, if I had been drowning and shouted to Suzy for help, she would have absentmindedly looked up from her book and said, "Okay, just let me finish this chapter," before putting her head back down. Meanwhile, Smokey slept in the dust at the side of the road. No fetching sticks in the lake for him. That was for amateurs.

When it was time to pack up and head home, we waited on the side of the road for a lift, hoping Ernie would pull over. When he did, we'd hustle into the cab, trailing wet towels and a dusty dog, smiling at our good fortune, and off we went, hurtling down the road.

If we got lucky, a log did tumble off the top of the load, bouncing us out of our seats in gales of laughter while Ernie merely glanced in the rear-view mirror and shouted, "We'll get 'er later," then slammed his foot on the gas.

Coming off the mountain, the road ran in a straight line across the valley floor to the dump, where the truckers could pick up speed, racing to get another load in before quitting time. And it was here, one day, roaring along with a cab full of kids that Ernie suddenly braked hard. The truck came to a shuddering halt, and he got out, shouting over his shoulder, "I'll be right back," and disappeared around the front of the truck.

"Do you think he hit something?" Suzy asked no one in particular.

"Yeah, and it's probably stuck in the grille," Franky replied with not a little bit of excitement in his voice.

"Well, why don't you get out and see what he's doing?" Wendy challenged him.

"No! He'll wring my neck!" Franky protested. Then he pointed out the window. "Look! He's gonna dump it in the bush."

Ernie had stepped off the road and was walking into the undergrowth, cradling something in his arms, and as he bent to place it on the ground, a tiny head peeked over his shoulder. Suzy gasped, "It's a fawn!" And sure enough, there it was, trembling and wide-eyed, watching Ernie as he made his way back through the undergrowth.

"I saw her lyin' there in the middle of the road and thought the next guy might run her over," Ernie explained, putting the truck in gear. "She's got my scent on her now, and the mother might not take her back, but we gave 'er a try, eh?" And with that, he lit a cigarette, and we took off.

Franky didn't know what to think. Like Suzy and Wendy and I, he was glad Ernie had rescued the fawn, but later on he wondered aloud, "What are the other guys gonna say if they find out?" With these conflicting ideas chasing each other around in his head, he began following Ernie around camp, sitting beside him in the cookhouse, and even copying the way he ate, like all the other ex-cons, with one hand wrapped around their plates, gripping their forks like a weapon. When Ernie poured Roger's Golden Syrup over his mashed potatoes, Franky followed suit, not really enjoying the taste but feeling as if he were doing the right thing.

After dinner, Ernie often stayed in the cookhouse to drink coffee and smoke, his big hands delicately laying loose tobacco along a cigarette paper, rolling it up and licking one edge as if he were sealing a tiny envelope. Then he lit up, took a drag, sat back, and relaxed for a few minutes before leaning forward to flick cigarette ash into one of his pant cuffs. "This is the polite way," he told Franky, "not like those guys who mess up nice clean ashtrays." Flick, flick, flick into the cuff went the ashes, and Franky waited for Ernie's pants to burst into flame, especially after a butt got dropped into the mix, but Ernie showed him that if your pants do catch fire, a little coffee poured directly into the cuff will set things right.

—⁕—

BY THE END OF THE SUMMER, THE AMERICAN BOATERS WERE back in Orford Bay, and they were always thrilled to be invited up the hill to watch trees crash to the ground. We'd send them off in the crummy[13] with Ernie behind the wheel, the men seated next to him with cameras in hand as if they were on safari, and the women in the back, smiling and waving.

Nobody mentioned that the crummy didn't have brakes, and when Franky asked his father if that was all right, he was told, "Well, as it turns out, Ernie's got some experience driving getaway cars, so if the crummy gets going too fast, he'll know what to do."

At the end of the day, the Yanks handed out cigarettes and chocolate, and when a pack of smokes was pressed into Ernie's hands, he didn't say much, just tossed it into the bush as soon as the visitors were out of sight.

"Why'd you do that?" Franky asked.

"Have you ever tasted American beer?" Ernie inquired, by way of reply. Franky said he hadn't. "Well," Ernie continued, "American

---

13   A vehicle used to transport loggers to work. In Orford Bay the *crummy* was a beat-up WWII jeep.

beer comes in fancy bottles and has no taste, and their cigarettes are the same kind of deal. The Yanks want everything to look perfect but things don't have to look good to be good," and with that he rolled another smoke and lit up.

Green Gold

Erik and Olaf Nyström were the best fallers on the coast. Smart logging contractors like Dad and Uncle Kurt were willing to pay them the astronomical rate of one hundred dollars a day, each, although Uncle Kurt said doling out that kind of money made him feel like he had to make up for it in other ways, like eating baloney sandwiches for dinner the rest of his life. In any case, hiring the Swedish siblings was money well spent; they saved Willcock & Wankel not only time but maybe a few lives as well, because falling trees was a damned dangerous business.

There was so much talk around camp about the Nyström brothers that I became convinced that, without them, our camp would shut down, raccoons would move into our house and sleep in our beds, and we'd have to go and live in a hotel on East Hastings Street—the kind with toilets down the hall.

However, Eric and Olaf returned to Orford Bay year after year, always arriving in camp with a flourish and style commensurate with their status as superstars of the logging industry. They'd sweep into the bay going a million miles an hour in their speedboat, throwing up a wash that sent all the boats tied to the float crashing into each other. But nobody seemed to mind. Their speedboat was called *Green Gold*, which Dad said had something to do with how much money they made. The instant they tied up to the stiff leg, Franky, Wendy, and I were there to fight over who got to carry their duffle bags into camp, confident the brothers welcomed us as their miniature sherpas as long as we didn't touch any of the precious equipment they had brought with them.

Wendy and I had been warned about a hundred times, and Franky twice as much, not to touch the brothers' exceptionally long power saws or, heaven forbid, their axes, which they kept in leather cases as if they were Stradivarius violins. Our parents were not worried that we might cut our hands off. More to the point, they were well aware that the fallers' saws and axes were irreplaceable, and if they got damaged, well, raccoons would be sitting at our kitchen table in no time at all.

Content to stagger up the stiff leg under the weight of the duffle bags, we followed the towering Vikings as they sauntered along ahead of us speaking to each other in Swedish, which, for me, was beyond worldly and romantic. At the end of the stiff leg, Dad and Uncle Kurt were there to greet them, shaking hands and welcoming them back to camp before the brothers went into the cookhouse to dine on thick steaks the cook prepared specially for them. Afterwards, they disappeared into the bunkhouse and climbed into beds Mum had made up with white cotton sheets and chenille bedspreads, each one adorned with a row of ladies in hoop skirts and bonnets dancing around the hem. The bedspreads were not the "exact" ones my mother had ordered from Eaton's catalogue but they were superior to the scratchy blankets the rest of the loggers had on their beds, clearly making the point that the Nyström brothers were just that much better than everyone else.

They stayed in camp about a week, cutting down trees, bucking off limbs, and leaving the logs where they fell for the loggers to go in and clean up over the next few months. They worked fast and efficiently and never had an accident. This was remarkable because there was no margin for error when falling old growth timber. Douglas firs can reach heights of over two hundred feet and measure six feet or more across at the butt, and when trees that size crash to the ground they often kick back or unexpectedly snap in two if there's rot in the trunk.

Consequently, fallers ran like hell to get out of the way the moment a tree began to topple. This was called "cut and run" in the logging industry, a phrase with a manly connotation in case anybody got ideas about loggers running scared.

On their last day in camp, the Swedish stars left more dramatically than they had arrived, looping round the bay not just once, but twice, before turning back to wave their goodbyes as the setting sun cast them in a golden glow. After they were gone, I was grateful we had once again been saved from raccoons and toilets down the hall.

Don't Chop Your Rope

CAMP SHUT DOWN IN THE WINTER. YOU CAN'T LOG WHEN THE forests are deep in snow, so that's when Dad came back home to our house in North Vancouver to relax and enjoy time with the family. This was fine and dandy, but sometimes he got a little antsy. I'd see him staring out a window, sizing up the trees in our backyard, and, predictably, he'd point one out and say, to no one in particular, "I think that tree there needs to be topped," and before you knew it, he was up the tree with his power saw. Luckily, the yard was full of evergreens so he always had something to do when things got a little dull around the house.

Except, once a tree was topped, he did a thing that caused a bit of a ruckus in the neighbourhood. He sat down. Not at the kitchen table. Not in front of the TV. Oh, no, he sat down to enjoy a bird's-eye view of his home and the surrounding area from the top of the tree he'd just whacked a few feet off. And that's when our phone would start ringing.

Now, most kids might feel that a father who sits on the top of a tree in the backyard is weird and embarrassing, but I didn't and neither did my sisters. When the neighbours called, we were amused. Mrs. Mathews was always the first to phone, and Wendy loved taking her calls. "Hello dear, this is. . . . Yes, that's right, Debbie's mum. . . . Yes, she is the one who knocked herself out twirling the baton. . . . She's fine, thank you. Now, I don't mean to be a pest, but I couldn't help noticing. . . . Yes, dear, she hit herself with quite a wallop, right between the eyes. . . . I just wanted you to know that your father. . . . Yes, like I said, dead-centre, but she'll be fine. . . . Anyhow, your father is sitting up in a tree again. I just wanted to make sure everything was all right. . . . Oh, so he's topping the tree? Yes, you probably did tell me that last time. Well, as long as everything is fine, dear. . . . You have a pleasant afternoon, too. Say hello to your Mum for me, and to your Dad, too. . . . when he comes down."

My father's tree topping antics were not just a result of his eccentricity (well, maybe a little). The thing was, he was a high rigger, like the professionals you see at loggers' sports shows who race up telephone poles, ring a bell, wave to the crowd, and race back down, all the while smiling and never breaking a sweat. Except that the poles Dad climbed were often more than a hundred and fifty feet tall. They were called spar trees, and climbing one of these giants involved plenty of sweat, but no waving or smiling, and definitely no bell-ringing.

Up until the 1960s, it was common practice for logging operations on the coast to have spar trees for hauling logs aerially. Stripped of branches and bark, the spar tree was rigged with cables that transported logs through the air and deposited them into a landing area, where they were loaded onto trucks. But before any of that could happen, the spar tree had to be topped for stability, and that's where the high rigger came in. And, to be clear, chopping the top off a tree may sound fairly straightforward, but most dangerous stuff does—otherwise, nobody would do it.

Starting out in the logging business in the 1930s, my father was an ideal high rigger, small and agile, with no fear of heights and a healthy fear of unemployment. Most loggers liked to keep their feet on the ground, so there were always jobs for high riggers as long as they had their own climbing equipment, which was really not asking a lot since the tools of the trade were basic: an axe, a pair of spurs with long spikes that were strapped to the medial side of the rigger's caulk boots, and a rope threaded through a wide leather belt that looped around the rigger and the spar tree.

The rigger progressed up the spar with crablike movements, kicking one spur after another deep into the wood while giving the rope enough slack to throw it higher and higher up the tree. On and on he went, and as the spar tapered out near the top, he shortened the length of his rope so he didn't lose his balance and fall backwards. In all, it took about an hour for a rigger to reach a point on the spar where it was about two feet in diameter. Here, he pulled out his axe and began chopping the top fifteen or twenty feet off, fully aware that one misplaced slice could cut through his rope, sending him to his death. Then, came the hard part. As the top of the tree plummeted to the ground, the spar began swaying like a blade of grass in the wind, back and forth, ten feet one way, ten feet the other, finding a new centre of gravity. After that, it was all downhill for the rigger, banging spurs into wood, looping the rope lower a hundred times over before he was finally back on *terra firma*—until the next day, when he was up the spar again, this time rigging it with cables. But it was all worth it, because high riggers got paid a few bucks more than the other loggers.

Later on, when Dad and Uncle Kurt had their own logging company, my father continued to do the high rigging. "It saves on flying in one of those high-priced young guys who think nothin' is ever gonna happen to them and they end up killing themselves," he reasoned. "I was young and stupid, but never reckless, and I guess that's why I'm still here."

Chapter Nine

Women's Work

The ice cream business, dance lessons for mean girls, and a recipe for baked starfish.

Waiting for the freight boat to dock. Mum is on the left.

BOAT DAY

EVERYBODY IN CAMP LOOKED FORWARD TO BOAT DAY, THE special day each month when a freight boat chugged into Orford Bay, stuffed to the gunwales with our food and supplies. In a way, it was like Christmas; orders were placed weeks ahead, then we waited to see what would be delivered. Sometimes we got what we asked for and sometimes we got something different. Either way, it was always a good day. If the cook ordered a case of pork chops, he might get lamb chops or ham hocks. Eaton's catalogue orders were pleasantly surprising or disappointing, depending upon your outlook on life. Order a pair of pedal pushers and you might get bicycle pedals or a push-up bra—both useful items given the right circumstances.

The freight boat schedule was also open to interpretation. It was supposed to arrive in Orford Bay on the fifteenth of every month, but sometimes it was a few days late due to bad weather or a breakdown. By then, the cookhouse was running low on food, and Dad sent us kids out fishing so the loggers could have something to eat for dinner besides Spam and canned peaches. When the freight boat finally did appear, everyone in camp dropped what they were doing, jumped into speedboats, and roared out to the float to pick up sacks of potatoes, boxes of frozen meat, crates of fresh fruit, cases of beer, truck tires, and, occasionally, an order of ice cream that inevitably came in a drippy cardboard box.

The freight boat was about a hundred feet long and equipped with a winch that lifted pallets of supplies onto the float. From there, everything was loaded into speedboats and motored across the bay to the stiff leg, where it was unloaded and carried up to the cookhouse. Barrels of gasoline were thrown over the side of the freight boat and towed to camp behind speedboats, but sometimes Wendy and Franky (the athletic ones) jumped into the saltchuck and pushed the barrels to shore through the bone-chilling water. It took about an hour before they crawled up the beach, covered head to toe in gasoline and close to hypothermic, but as most parents would agree, you gotta keep kids busy. Otherwise, they might get into trouble doing some really dangerous stuff.

If the tide was low, supplies were carried into camp along a shoreline trail for about a quarter of a mile, each crate and box balanced high on the men's shoulders. At times like this, I was grateful we were in a camp of burly loggers and not skinny accountants, an opinion based solely on my parents' accountant who was so scrawny Dad said it was a good thing he only ever had to lift pieces of paper.

Food orders had to be precise and well thought out, each meal planned down to the last piece of pie and baloney sandwich; there was no running to the corner store to pick up forgotten items because there was no corner store. Meat was especially tricky to order since there was no refrigeration in camp, and meal planning was done according to how fast meat defrosted and began to go off. The cook wrote up the food order each month and handed it to my mother who immediately began crossing out items she thought were too extravagant, or simply ridiculous, like Jell-O, which for Mum was a non-starter. "Men do not like Jell-O," she firmly stated. "It's a waste of their time." However, she was wise enough to understand that loggers depended on good grub because there wasn't much else to do in camp besides eat and think about what you were going to eat, so she kept the orders pretty much intact. And, not to put too fine a point on it, she didn't want to piss off the cook, because he might quit and she would be next up to bat in the cookhouse. That thought alone was worth leaving all the roasts of beef on the order.

When Mum wasn't in camp, the food bills were always high because the orders were left to my father to check, and he didn't know much about food besides how to eat it. For instance, he had no clue that it wasn't necessary to order a case of vanilla extract every month unless you owned a bakery in Paris, or were an alcoholic, since pure vanilla extract is around 40 percent alcohol.

Mum figured out the cook was drinking vanilla extract the day she was placing a food order via radio telephone, laboriously reciting each item into the receiver by name, brand and quantity: "One 50 pound sack of Robin Hood flour, over. . . . Three cases of Carnation Evaporated Milk, over. . . . Eight grade A roasts of beef, 10 pounds each, over. . . . twelve 24 ounce bottles of vanilla extract, over. . . ." Wait a minute! How had she missed this? It was outrageous, and she'd put a stop to it immediately! Then she reconsidered. The cook was always in a pretty good mood, so maybe a few extra bottles of vanilla extract were not such a big deal after all.

The most precious item that landed on the dock was the mailbag, a big canvas sack emblazoned with the words "Royal Mail" along with an image of a crown, reminders that the Queen would not be amused if you fooled around with her mailbag. In any case, on Boat Day, the mail was what the loggers looked forward to more than the rest of us. They got letters from home, *Playboy* magazines, and newspapers, the special things they needed to relieve the loneliness and boredom of camp life. Unfortunately, on one particularly blustery Boat Day, I was carrying the mailbag along the stiff leg when I lost my balance and fell in, bag and all.

Most of the guys were nice about getting wet mail. I remember loggers sitting on the boardwalk peeling apart the soggy pages of their letters, and I felt kind of bad about that, especially when Ernie, never one to have unexpressed thoughts about my behaviour, told me the letter from his wife was in such rough shape he wasn't sure if she was leaving the following week for Manitoba or leaving him for a man who played the tuba. Holding the wet pages of the letter out in front of him, he looked me straight in the eye and said, "I guess if I don't get a letter next Boat Day, I'll know she took off with the musician."

While the crew looked forward to getting mail, we kids wanted ice cream, and the best part of getting it was that we had to eat it right away, otherwise it would melt. There was always more than enough for everybody in camp, though Mum never joined in the feeding frenzy. She said it was because of what happened when we were little kids and still in diapers.

Back then, she was washing the laundry by hand, including cloth diapers for Wendy and me. This is not a task for the faint of heart. First, she boiled water on the woodstove, then she poured it into a galvanized tub she kept on the back porch. But you don't just throw dirty diapers into a tub of hot soapy water, you got to get the worst of the business off first. For this unpleasant, but necessary, task she used an old butcher knife. It really was the most efficient tool for kind of scraping . . . well, use your imagination. She kept the knife stuck into a tree at the back of our house.

Then one hot summer day, the freight boat arrived, and Uncle Kurt was thrilled to discover a box containing several cartons of ice cream, but they were melting fast. He raced back to camp with the limp box and quickly assembled all the loggers into our backyard to partake of this special treat. He ripped open the cartons and began slicing generous slabs of ice cream for everyone with a knife he had found stuck into a nearby tree. He was doling out ice cream as fast as he could to the crowd gathered round him when Mum arrived back home. She said everyone looked so happy: it was a beautiful day, the diapers on the clothesline were fluttering in the breeze, and everyone was digging into the ice cream like nobody's business. So she decided on the spot that she was not going to tell them whose "business" they were digging into. It was like Christmas, sometimes you get what you ask for, and sometimes you get something different. Either way, it was a good day.

Nanaimo Bars

ALMOST EVERYTHING IN CAMP ATTRACTED BEARS. SWEATY work socks were irresistible, caulk boots were nice and chewy, and coffee thermoses had a satisfying crunch. However, it was the cookhouse that really got a bear's olfactory senses revving with the aromas of raw meat and buckets of lard, not to mention the cook who always smelled absolutely delicious. All it took was a mere whiff of this rare cuisine, and a bear was hooked. Nothing could scare them away: yelling, banging on pots and pans, getting Smokey to try and bark them to death, or firing warning shots over their heads. None of this gave them the slightest hint they were not welcome in camp. In fact, they acted a lot like out-of-town guests, the kind who drop in uninvited, eat everything in sight, and leave you with a big mess to clean up.

Most logging camps like ours kept rifles on hand for shooting problem bears. It was not a sport; we just couldn't let them tear the camp apart or eat any of us. There were two rifles in Orford Bay, a powerful hunting rifle and a .22 that was considered a kind of toy because Franky and I were allowed to use it for target practice (which also proves I was not my parents' favourite child). My sisters and I knew the hunting rifle meant business, because we had a hole in our kitchen floor the size of a pie plate from the time Dad was giving one of the loggers a lesson in gun safety and didn't realize the gun was loaded.

If a bear was shot in Orford Bay, several loggers hauled it down to the beach, and from there, it was towed out to deep water and dumped. As callous as this sounds, it was the best way to get rid of the carcass. It couldn't be simply left to rot, because that would attract other bears and a host of smaller scavengers.

One summer, a young black bear took up residence in camp and would not leave. It had most likely been orphaned and hadn't yet learned to fend for itself. No matter how many times Smokey chased it out of camp, it appeared again the next day and soon became fearless, going so far as to stroll into the bunkhouse one Sunday afternoon when the loggers were taking it easy. They panicked, yelling and throwing boots and ashtrays at the terrified animal. It scrambled through a window, leaving behind a trail of broken glass and several Playmate of the Month pin-ups mauled beyond recognition.

It was clear the bear had to go, and later that afternoon Dad shot it. I helped him tie it to the back of a speedboat, and as we motored out of the bay, I leaned over the stern holding the front paws in my hands to keep it from getting tangled in the rope. The pads on its feet were soft and the claws reached partway up my forearms. When we reached the deepest part of the bay, we untied it, then motored back to camp in silence.

That same summer, Franky and I built a fort in a big stump that had washed up on the beach in front of our house. It was an architectural masterpiece, constructed out of driftwood and broken boards, featuring three rickety floors connected by an interior ladder. Franky claimed the top floor because he said he needed a lookout, but I knew he sat up there and ate a stash of Nanaimo bars he kept in a tin under the floorboards—something we both knew could attract bears.

Early one morning, after the loggers had left for work, we heard Smokey barking like crazy. This wasn't unusual, though the barking continued for longer than it ordinarily took him to scare a deer or raccoon out of camp, so we knew there was a bear nearby doing what bears usually did: wandering around camp looking for something to eat. Smokey versus bear dramas usually fizzled out when the bear moved off on its own accord and Smokey came home and collapsed on the front porch. So that morning, my sisters and I continued reading our novels and enjoying our bowls of Corn Flakes, confident that things would soon calm down.

However, Smokey did not let up. Without looking up from her book, Suzy suggested that Wendy go take a look at what was going on outside, but she refused, saying that it wasn't her turn and that, if she remembered correctly, it was actually my turn. I got up from the table before remembering that we didn't take turns for stuff like this, but by then I was committed. I shuffled over to the front door and poked my head out. "Come here quick!" I yelled at my sisters who reluctantly got up from the table to join me. A grizzly was ripping the fort apart! The bear had its back to us and was standing on its hind legs, tossing boards over its shoulders like a Canada Customs agent going through a suitcase.

I knew right away that it was the stash of Nanaimo bars that had attracted the bear, but I kept quiet, deciding it was not the right time to share that information. Meanwhile, Smokey was lunging at the bear, barking like crazy, and dodging and ducking each time the grizzly turned around to swat at him. Mum joined us on the porch to see what all the ruckus was about, knitting in one hand and a cup of coffee in the other. Taking one look at the bear she exclaimed, "Holy Moses!" which in Mum-speak meant "What the #@&*!" She ordered everyone back inside, grabbed hold of the hunting rifle we kept in a corner of the kitchen, and began inserting bullets into the chambers, all the while reminding Suzy to take the bread out of the oven if she wasn't back in half an hour.

From the kitchen window, we watched our mother walk down the porch steps and out into the grassy field in front of our house, never taking her eyes off the grizzly. When she found a good sightline, she lifted the rifle to her shoulder, peered through the scope, and began to fire over the bear's head, one shot after another, trying to scare it off. However, with each shot the bear merely paused, glanced at my mother, and went right back to ransacking the fort. It didn't take long for Mum to run out of patience; she had better things to do, and as she reached into her apron pocket for one more bullet, she had a change of mind. It was time for the angry mother voice, the one we all know. "Go on!" she shouted. "Don't make me tell you again, or you'll be sorry! I'll put a bullet right through your head!" And with that brief, succinct scolding, the grizzly stopped, turned to take one last look at Mum, and ambled off into the bush—just like that.

Modern Inconveniences

QUEEN FOR A DAY WAS A POPULAR TV GAME SHOW IN THE 1960s that featured downtrodden housewives who were allotted sixty seconds each to tell their tales of woe. The woman deemed to have the life that sucked the most was selected *Queen for a Day* and paraded around the stage wearing a crown and a robe while weeping tears of joy. Her grand prize for having the most tragic life that day was usually a washing machine or a refrigerator, while the runners-up got less grand items, such as electric carving knives, which probably came in real handy when slicing baloney.

Now, by today's standards, awarding women household appliances is considered sexist and a whole lot of other words that end with "ist." I have to agree, but I loved that show and wished with all my heart that Mum could be one of the contestants because she legitimately did need some new appliances in Orford Bay—and I could really have used a crown and a robe.

—◦—

WHEN WE FIRST CAME TO ORFORD BAY MY MOTHER DID ALL THE laundry by hand, using a washboard and a bar of Sunlight soap the size of a brick, scrubbing until her arms were chapped up to the elbows.

The washing got hung on a clothesline in the backyard, but when it rained, wet clothes were draped over a laundry rack above the wood-stove, taking on the aromas of bacon, coffee, and homemade bread. After that, Mum got out her flat irons, which she heated on the stove-top, wary of their arbitrary temperature settings, which amounted to "Hot," "Scorch Your Clothes," and "Melt the Skin Off Your Hands."

Aunty Patty tried convincing my mother that her Coleman Instant-Lite Model 4A Gas Iron was a big improvement on the flat irons, but she wouldn't budge, complaining that the Instant-Lite had most likely been invented by a man who liked sharp creases in his pants more than he liked his wife's eyebrows, and she was not far wrong. The Instant-Lite ran on gasoline and came equipped with a small tank that bore a disturbing resemblance to a hand grenade. Lighting the iron resulted in it momentarily bursting into flame before settling down to an evil hiss. Mum was having none of that.

Combustible irons aside, Mum did succumb to the lure of light-ening her workload after Ivor, a light-fingered beachcomber, chugged into camp one morning with a wringer washer upside down in the stern of his skiff. Mum welcomed him, but made no offer of coffee, because the last time he was in the house, the binoculars went missing.

"Now, Joanie," he said, leaning against the upturned legs of the washer, "I'm gonna let you have this washer here for twenty bucks, which I fully understand, more than most, may seem a bit on the high side. However," he added, his index finger pointing heavenward, "I know quality when I see it, and this little baby's got a real skookum motor. And, I don't want to pressure you," he went on, his finger now raised to biblical heights, "but that old Swede's wife at the place around the point offered me twenty-five bucks for her. But I like you, Joanie, and since you got all them kids, I just want to help you out."

Mum eyed Ivor, undeceived. But contemplating the endless stream of work clothes and other laundry, she decided the wringer washer had to be better than a washboard. She handed over the cash, and Ivor flipped the washer onto the float right side up.

It was installed in the tool shed, hooked up to the generator, and Mum set to work, overjoyed with the anticipation of automation, though she did have some concerns that one of us kids (Franky) might get his fingers caught in the wringer and end up with an arm resembling the business end of a canoe paddle. But, turning her attention back to the laundry sloshing around all by itself, she felt her elbows getting smoother by the minute.

Granted, the wringer washer was nothing like the machines on *Queen for a Day,* but it did the job. Her only complaint was that it occasionally exploded—not enough to send her flying across Orford Bay, but enough to shred the laundry and scare the bejesus out of her.

The problem had to do with the fact that Dad was the explosives "expert" in camp, a position he took on only because the other guys could not be convinced that having a lit cigarette in your mouth while igniting sticks of dynamite was not conducive to staying alive. Though dynamite by itself did not really give you much of a bang for your buck, it was the detonators, called "blasting caps," that really got things off the ground. They were about the size of a shirt button and were used to ignite the dynamite loggers used when building access roads. Wendy and Franky and I found they made excellent substitutes for poker chips. Dad just told us not to bang them around too much.

Every morning, my father left the house with a handful of blasting caps in his pants pocket in case he had to blow anything up at work that day. Later, when he got home, he occasionally forgot to take the spare caps out of his pockets before throwing them into the laundry. Once the caps got into the washer and were caught under the agitator, the pressure was enough to set them off. And that set Mum off.

"KABOOM!" The sound of an explosion in the tool shed sent her rushing out the front door to turn the washer off and retrieve what was left of Dad's pants. Usually, just one pocket was blown out. Other times, the pants got pulled out of the washer looking like Bermuda shorts, but only on one leg. After Mum's heart rate returned to normal, she felt around inside the tub for any more caps before feeding the clothes through the wringer, but occasionally an undetected cap got squished between the rollers and "KABOOM!!!" Eventually the tub in the washer became so dented and cracked that it no longer rotated, and Mum returned to the safety of her washboard.

Years later, the camp was sold to a big logging corporation. They got rid of all the houses and moved in trailers for the loggers to live in. There was also a washhouse equipped with modern steam irons nobody used, and washing machines, like the ones on *Queen for A Day*, and the loggers confirmed what they had always suspected: doing laundry was actually quite easy.

Just Relax

WHILE MUM WAS WRESTLING WITH WASHING MACHINES, SUZY, Wendy, and I were at Dotty's house, wallowing on her couch with bags of potato chips and piles of trashy magazines. She was our "fun" aunt, and when she was in camp, her house was the place to hang out. She didn't know the first thing about kids, but she taught us some valuable life skills, like how to make what she called a "decent" dry martini and apply eyeliner with a black felt pen, "in case you're out all night and have to go to work straight from the bar." I wished my mother had some of her panache, though Franky thought his mother was just an ordinary mum. He made her laugh, and she let him do whatever he wanted, and it all worked out just fine—most of the time.

Dotty had a poker table set up in one corner of her kitchen, and our games went on for days, though Suzy and I didn't play as much as Wendy and Franky because we were more interested in reading Dotty's steamy paperbacks. Her sister sent the novels all the way from California, in brown paper wrappers no less, and the fact that I couldn't understand the risqué language did not diminish the pleasure I got from reading books that would have set my mother's hair on fire had she found out.

The best part about being at Dotty's house was our dance lessons. We practiced the rhumba, the cha-cha, and the quickstep to songs like

"Itsy Bitsy Teenie Weenie Yellow Polka Dot Bikini," singing the lyrics because we didn't have a record player. Dotty danced around with a cigarette in one hand and a drink in the other, and we followed along as she directed us between refrains of "Itsy Bitsy" and other catchy tunes, "Now, one, two, cha, cha, cha, three, four, cha, cha, cha . . . yes, you've got it, cha, cha, cha, that's right, cha, cha, cha, watch your hands . . . just relax. . . ."

Meanwhile, Mum was encouraging us girls to learn how to embroider pillowcases for our hope chests and tie reef knots for Girl Guide badges. But we were having none of it and shunned her like a pack of mean girls, slinking home at dinnertime to eat the food she had prepared, then dashing out the door to Dotty's to play a few more hands of Seven Card Stud until it was lights out.

However, as much as we loved having Dotty in camp, she was always looking for any excuse, valid or not, to go back to Vancouver where she found life a little more stimulating than dancing around her kitchen with a bunch of kids. She never came right out and said she wanted to leave; instead, she might have an "accident," like the time she "sprained her ankle" and Uncle Kurt had to carry her around camp on his back for a few days until she could get a plane out. The minute the Beaver landed, however, she sprinted towards it as if she were the front runner in an Olympic final.

A far more expedient way for her to get to Vancouver was to flip out, and it didn't take much to set her off, such as a bat flying around her bedroom or a banana slug on her toothbrush. She'd throw her head back and let out a howl, rivalling the wolf calls we heard at night. This was Dotty's way of letting us know she couldn't cope with camp life any longer, and if having a fit got her the hell out of camp, I suppose that was exactly what she needed.

In Vancouver, she quickly got back in her groove. Most nights she was out with her friends, tearing up the dance floors all over town, and during the day she loved to shop. She bought designer dresses before most Canadian women even knew there was such a thing. Her spending sprees did not stop there. One of her more interesting purchases was a player piano, the dumbest invention in the world. It looked like a regular upright piano but nobody played it because it did all the plonk-plonking for you. I never understood the point of it. Anyhow, I think Dotty got it cheap because it was upholstered in shiny gold vinyl—and that's the truth.

She also liked to buy pets and always had some kind of feathered or furry creature in a cage. She started with hamsters, and when they escaped, she moved on to a Myna bird that spit sunflower seeds all over the kitchen when it wasn't making a racket that sounded as if someone with laryngitis was being strangled. Then there was the chihuahua puppy she bought to keep her company, which it did, until the cat ate it, leaving its tiny bones scattered across the living room carpet. When I told Dad about the untimely death of "Burrito," he agreed that it was a real tragedy but assured me the burial would be a cinch.

Back in the city, Dotty was a great hostess, often inviting other loggers' wives over to play bridge, and when it came to impressing the ladies, a seven-layer chocolate "Dream Cake" was just the thing. One time, Franky and I watched her make one of these towering marvels from start to finish, and when she was done, she slid it into her oh-so-modern refrigerator with the revolving Lazy Susan shelves, warning us not to go near it while she went out to pick up a few things before "the girls" arrived.

Dutifully, Franky and I distanced ourselves from the cake and went outside to play. But after about an hour, we were thirsty and ran inside for a drink. Franky went straight for the fridge, yanked the door open and spied a jug of orange juice on the shelf behind the cake, and before I could say, "Watch ooooout. . . ." he gave that lazy Susan a spin like it was a Las Vegas roulette wheel, propelling the cake out of the fridge and onto the kitchen floor in a heap. And that's when we heard Dotty's Cadillac pull into the driveway. A few minutes later the howling started, and it went on for a really long time, enough to put any wolf to shame.

Finally recovering her composure, she poured herself a drink, lit a cigarette, and surveyed the remains of the "Dream Cake." Then she calmly told Franky to get some spoons and we all got down on our hands and knees and scooped the sticky mess off the floor and into Dotty's best crystal bowl. "The girls" were going to have an English trifle for dessert—possibly with a few sunflower seeds thrown into the mix. The floor got washed, Dotty changed into one of her swishy dresses, and just before the bridge ladies arrived, she turned to Franky and me with a menacing smile on her face and said, "If either of you two little buggers breathe a word about what happened here today, I'll wring your necks. Now, go play."

BUSTED

MY MOTHER WROTE LETTERS. IF SHE HAD A PROBLEM FOR WHICH no solution could be found in either the *Encyclopedia Britannica* or the *Joy of Cooking*, she fired off a letter, trusting that somewhere out there was a smart man who would tell her what she needed to do. Likewise, she did her part to keep the country running on an even keel, writing letters of advice and guidance to those suffering from moral dilemmas or stupidity. The prime minister received a letter informing him that he was behaving like a jackass in case nobody else had told him, Mr. Eaton got a letter telling him that the quality of his cotton brassieres wasn't what it used to be, and her letter to a bishop of the Anglican Church made it clear that "Onward Christian Soldiers" was a perfectly fine hymn and should not be removed from the otherwise dull-as-dishwater repertoire of hymns normally sung in church.

She wrote with a fountain pen and used her best stationery, believing that her letters were important and that she shouldn't mess around with pencils and lined paper if she wanted to be taken seriously. That's how my mother rolled: an answer to every question, a solution to every problem—at least that was her theory until the waterline busted.

The original waterline ran for a couple of miles, emerging from the depths of a pool in the Orford River, way back in the valley, and snaking along a bushwhacked trail, over tree roots, around boulders, and under logs before arriving in camp. But the hose was showing signs of wear and had even sprung a leak or two, so Mum thought it was prudent to replace it before any serious problems occurred.

The "Best Value Premium Hose" she purchased early one spring from McDonald & McGrath, Manufacturers of Superior Waterlines Ltd. promised to be "kink resistant," "crush resistant," "tested to the highest industry standards," and "guaranteed for life." It was shipped via Royal Mail from Toronto and arrived in Orford Bay in record time, an improvement in service my mother took as a clear indication that her letter to the Postmaster General had not fallen on deaf ears.

The new waterline was laid down, hooked up, and then all hell broke loose. It continuously broke, tore, and pulled apart, causing the faucets in camp to erupt, spewing mud and debris as if the bowels of the earth were dealing with bad oysters. This often occurred when the loggers were showering, and we could hear them beseeching God, Jesus, and Christ Almighty to help get the soap out of their eyes before they gave up on divine intervention and jumped into the saltchuck to rinse off. If the line burst when the men were at work, my mother and Aunty Patty had to do the repairs since they were the only adults in camp during the day, except for the cook, and he was too busy complaining about the water being cut off to be of much help.

Repairing the waterline was usually just a matter of pulling handfuls of gunk out of the hose or patching a tear with rubberized canvas, glue, and a few clamps. However, around the middle of August that year, unprecedented summer rainstorms pounded the south coast, and they didn't let up until the unprecedented rains of autumn began.

The loggers left for work every morning in oilskins and came home at the end of the day soaked to the bone. They were working longer days than usual, spending much of their time repairing washed-out roads, and that left Mum and Aunty Patty fully responsible for the waterline. Time after time, the hose floated off the trail, wrapping around tree trunks and twisting into Gordian knots they cut apart rather than attempting to untangle. And if that wasn't bad enough, late August was the time the grizzlies lined up along the banks of the river to gorge on salmon and fatten up for the coming winter. So, repairs to the waterline required a rifle, and that was a problem for Aunty Patty.

"I just don't think your aim is that good," she confessed to my mother. "I've seen your photo albums, Joan, and the thought of all those people without heads doesn't make me feel real relaxed when you're packin' that gun."

All the same, duty called, and day after day they geared up and headed into the woods with my mother in the lead, rifle at the ready. She was unwilling to relinquish the gun, telling Dad that his sister was too much of a freethinker to be trusted with a weapon and, come to think of it, equally unqualified to be a judge of anyone's photography.

On one particularly wet day early in September, they were unable to find the problem on the line and continued trekking deep into the valley until they reached the river's edge. There, Aunty Patty pulled the hose out of the pool to discover the intake valve was choked with dirt. It only took a few minutes to set things right, but as they were about to set out for home, Mum nudged Aunty Patty, whispering, "Don't move. I think I heard something," and a moment later, an enormous grizzly stepped out of the forest on the opposite side of the river.

Rising into the air as one, they pivoted in the direction of camp, their legs racing, cartoon-style, as they took off down the trail. It was every woman for herself. Mum was in the lead for a few minutes, but when she slipped and fell, Aunty Patty sailed over her like an Olympic hurdler, both legs lifted horizontally in perfect formation. On they raced, jockeying back and forth, elbowing each other out of the way, until they finally were back in camp, covered in mud and gasping for air.

Trying to catch her breath, Aunty Patty turned to Mum and wheezed, "Okay . . . we got lucky that time . . . the bear didn't get us . . . and you didn't shoot me, but I'm not doin' that again. I quit."

"Don't worry," Mum gasped, taking in great gulps of air. "I'll write a letter."

It was one of her finest epistles. In the confines of the six pages she referred to as her "Toronto Letter," my mother demanded, in no uncertain terms, that McDonald & McGrath, Manufacturers of Superior

Tubing and Waterlines Ltd. replace the "Best Value Premium Hose" for a much-better-value premium hose. Furthermore, she also suggested a general rethinking of the morality of selling a hose that was not worthy of its guarantees. Then she sat back and waited, and waited, until it became clear that this was a hell-freezing-over kind of wait.

Suzy suggested she phone the company to which our mother replied, "Don't be ridiculous. Nobody phones anybody in Toronto. You can't just phone Toronto," but then she did some general rethinking of her own and decided that phoning Toronto was exactly what she was going to do. Putting her pen and paper aside, Mum prepared to make a "long-distance call," and she was up for the challenge.

She got hold of the telephone number, carefully calculated the time difference and the long-distance charges, and called Mr. McDonald and Mr. McGrath, fully prepared to tell them a thing or two. The call went something like this: "Hello? Hello? Oh, hello, there you are. I'm calling from British Columbia. Can you hear me? Oh, oh, that's good. I can hear you, too. This is Mrs. Willcock, and I'm calling about our waterline in Orford Bay, that's on the coast here. Which type of line? Well, it's black, and there's a picture of it in your catalogue. Oh, you just answer the phones? You want me to wait and you will transfer me? This call is costing. . . . Oh, Hello, this is Mrs. Willcock, and . . . yes, our waterline. It's in your catalogue on page . . . just a sec, I've got it right here. Page twelve, right at the top there, the 'Best Value Premium' one. Oh! You work in the warehouse? Oh, I am sorry about that. Yes, I'm sure they should pay you to know about every single item on the shelves. Well, thank you. . . . Could you do a telephone transfer to another person who might be able to. . . . Hello?"

The waterline was never replaced, we just got better clamps and bigger patches. Meanwhile, Mum began to loosen her grip on a few things, occasionally allowing Aunty Patty to carry the gun (never letting on that it wasn't loaded), and she also accepted the fact there was not an answer to every question or a solution to every problem—but she remained convinced that phoning anyone in Toronto was a complete waste of time.

Beyoudyful

AUNTY PATTY WAS NOTHING LIKE MY MOTHER. SHE WAS SPON-
taneous and eccentric. In the summer, she gardened in her underwear
because "you can't beat a good pair of cotton undies for keeping you cool
on a hot day." For a more formal look, she took down her living room
curtains and whipped up a lovely dress and matching jacket. When
Ruby and Donna weren't in camp, I had her all to myself, and we spent
every spare moment together creating what she called "beyoudyful"
works of art. That's how I found out the world was brimming with pos-
sibility. I just had to know where to look.

When Aunty Patty and Uncle Floyd were back home in Lund,
she found work shucking oysters and cutting salal for florist shops in
Vancouver, and he worked as a gillnetter. Despite the fact they didn't
have much money, they had a beautiful home because Aunty Patty was
"repurposing" and "recycling" before those words were made up to
make people feel better about being poor. However, she legitimately
loved giving old things a new life, like the pile of second-hand coats
she braided into a living room rug, or the whale vertebra she found
on the beach and hung over the fireplace, the sharp processes radi-
ating out from it like a fossilized star. After completing a project, she
would stand back admiring her work and say, "Don't you think it's just
beyoudyful?" For me, her projects were more than "beyoudyful"; they

were freedom of expression, and I wanted some of that.

In camp, the first time we worked together as a team was when we painted her kitchen cupboards. We started on the uppers, then did the lowers, and didn't stop when we got to the fridge, which also got a nice coat of paint. After that, the gloves were off. I was forever running from Aunty Patty's house to my own, flinging the door open and breathlessly asking my mother if she had specific items we needed for a project, like plastic flowers, a tobacco can, or some blue food dye. The only time Mum questioned what we were up to was when I asked for a blowtorch; otherwise she'd just say, "Uh-huh, hold on a sec," then hand over what I'd asked for. Then I'd run all the way back to Aunty Patty's, afraid I might have missed something in the five minutes I'd been gone.

We created mobiles out of clamshells and fishing line, and poured sealing wax into plump moon shells to make candles. Gnarled tree roots were pulled out of the riverbed and polished with floor wax to create what she called, "real interesting sculptures." At other times, she and I sat on the kitchen floor sewing beach bags from burlap potato sacks we got from the cookhouse, embroidering flowers on each bag with fat strands of darning wool. I was in heaven.

Her bathroom renovation was a particularly complex project that took up a few weeks of our time one summer. She said, "I want something inspirational to look at while I'm doing my business," so we wallpapered the bathroom with "beachy" pictures cut from old magazines. However, the renovation would not have been complete without a few starfish tastefully suspended from the ceiling in a piece of fishnet, and that's when things got what she called "not foreseed."

Now, to most people, it's fairly obvious that you have to dry starfish before they can be used as works of art. After all, nobody wants slimy starfish hanging from their bathroom ceiling. But not being someone to hesitate when she had the creative spark, Aunty Patty ran to the beach, grabbed a few dozen starfish, and popped them in the oven, saying she could "dry them out in a jiffy."

But baking starfish was not easy. They started out smelling a bit fishy, then really fishy, and soon, gas-mask fishy. We flung open all the doors and windows in the house to prevent asphyxiation, and before long a starfish smog hung over Orford Bay. When the loggers arrived back in camp later that afternoon, they paused, looking this way and that for a dead animal washed up on the beach.

Uncle Floyd took the whole episode in stride. He called the smell "Eau de Low Tide," adding that he was going to have to sleep with the windows open, "for the not forseed future." Aunty Patty also got over the incident quickly, though she couldn't get the stench out of her oven and had to ask a couple of the loggers to dump the stove on the beach where it quickly became home to a whole lot of starfish.

A more successful project was the rag dolls we stitched together from fabric scraps, then stuffed so tight they were as dense as punching bags. Dad said the next time he had to fire a logger he would take one of our dolls with him in case he got into a fight and needed a weapon. But they were pretty. We gave them big brown eyes and dark wool hair parted in the middle. They wore white aprons over simple cotton dresses, and Aunty Patty said they reminded her of a photograph of my grandmother taken shortly before she was sent off to residential school.

Years later, when I was working in Japan, I got the news that Aunty Patty had died. I was broken-hearted and disappointed that I hadn't had a chance to say goodbye. But one day, strolling through an antique market awash in brilliant kimonos, I felt her beside me, whispering in my ear that everything was just so "beyoudyful."

Do as She Pleased

THE VILLAGE OF LUND WAS STILL ENVELOPED IN DARKNESS WHEN
Ruby tiptoed out the back door. Nigel-the-neighbour's chickens weren't
even up, and Aunty Patty and Donna wouldn't rouse for a few hours
yet. The only sound came from the waves below the house, sliding up
and down the beach like the ticking of a clock, and Ruby quickened
her steps towards the garden shed where her bicycle lay in the grass.
Pulling it upright she flicked the slugs off the handlebars, swiped the
dew off the seat, and set off.

It would take her two hours to get to Powell River. The first car
ferry of the day hadn't docked at Saltery Bay yet, and she had the road
to herself. The only distractions at this hour were skittering rodents
that didn't bother to look both ways and squashed garter snakes that
she recoiled from, instinctively lifting her feet off the pedals.

She was confident she'd arrive at the Motor Vehicle Department
office before it opened, assuring herself first place in line for her driver's test, even though she knew nobody else would line up behind
her. In fact, there had never been a lineup of any sort in Powell River,
except for the annual rummage sale at St. Christopher's and the
liquor store on New Year's Eve. However, today was her birthday, July
6, 1961, and she didn't want to waste a moment of her sixteenth year
not having the legal authority to go anywhere she wanted and do as
she pleased.

She already had a plan for where she would drive once she got her licence, but as she pedalled along it gave her pleasure to go over it in her head one more time. The first stop would be the Dairy Queen in Powell River. She was going to park right out front, get a milkshake, and drive off holding it in one hand with the other on the wheel, or maybe just her index finger would do the steering, though she wasn't sure how easy that would be. On Sunday, she would drive to church, parking perfectly between the lines, open the driver's door, and swing both legs out together because that's what you did when you drove a car and wore a dress at the same time. Saving the best for last, she saw herself cruising down the road to the Lund Hotel for ice cream. It was only a ten-minute walk from her house, but what the hell, she could do as she pleased. She'd pull up in front of the hotel like the tourists did on their way to Savary Island, leaving their engines running while they dashed inside to grab ice cream cones, and she imagined herself doing the same—like it was no big deal.

Mr. Doupe, her Geography teacher, was the Motor Vehicle Department examiner. It was his summer job, and he made sure to ask each applicant the name of the roads and landmarks around Powell River. "In case you get yourself turned around one day and don't know how the hell to get home," he cautioned, dropping in the "hell" so it was understood he was Mr. Doupe, the driving examiner, and not Mr. Doupe, the teacher.

Ruby made short work of the test, passing all the requirements except for parallel parking. "But everyone from Lund has trouble with that," Mr. Doupe reassured her. "I suppose it's because you can park almost in the middle of the road there and nobody seems to mind." Licence in hand, she pedalled back home, hoping that Nigel-the-neighbour would be around. She wanted to talk to him about buying his car since her family did not own a vehicle of any description.

"I'll sell her to you for fifty bucks," Nigel told Ruby. "She's British-made and rock-solid. We brought her over with us. Got her right after the war and she ran like an absolute dream until we parked her here."

The Morris Minor was really more of a chicken coop than a motor vehicle. However, Nigel assured Ruby that "she'll be as good as new once Gladys and the girls move out," referring to his favourite hen and her entourage. The other problem with the car was that both headlights were smashed in. Years earlier, Nigel had stopped driving the Morris after he plowed into the back of a car one night on Finn Bay Road. He said he hadn't expected some idiot to have parked almost in the middle of the road but, truth be told, Nigel had been driving without the Morris's headlights turned on, like he always did to extend the life of the battery.

"That's what makes the car even more of a bargain," he assured Ruby, "the battery is almost brand new." He pounded his fist on the hood of the car to emphasize its worthiness, coming away with it dripping in white glop, which he then wiped on his pant leg with a grimace, adding: "I'll get her cleaned up, and when you come back in August, you can pay me."

For the past two summers, Ruby and Donna had remained in Lund under the supervision of Nigel-the-neighbour and his wife Priscilla while Aunty Patty joined Uncle Floyd in camp. Both the girls were complete dunces in geography and had been obliged to attend summer school to study (again) what Mr. Doupe called "the physical makeup of the earth," and Donna referred to as "stuff I don't want to know." Aunty Patty figured Mr. Doupe had taken the job at the Motor Vehicle office just to avoid her daughters, and she really couldn't blame him.

This year, however, the girls were coming to camp as soon as school let out. "Your sister needs cheering up," she told Ruby, "and I think it would be fun if we were all together in Orford Bay." But Aunty Patty was lying, as all good mothers must do from time to time. The truth was she was worried that if Donna remained in Lund she might take off for California to try and rekindle her romance with "Chip the surfer." Aunty Patty knew her daughter didn't really know where California was, but she was confident Donna could find a Greyhound bus driver who did.

Chip and Donna had met the summer before on the tea cups ride at Disneyland. He didn't actually know how to surf, but that was okay with Donna, because "he looks like he could if he'd wanted to," she told Ruby, referring to his tan and flip-flops. It had been love at first spin, and they had written to each other for over nine-and-three-quarters months. But he had broken up with her in his latest letter, stating that it had all been a mistake, and how was he to know she wasn't Swedish like that actress in the movie who goes into the fountain and gets her dress all wet. He had looked up Lund in the *American Atlas* and found out there was only one—in Sweden—and honestly, he felt a little cheated.

Having been defeated by geography once again, Donna took up position on the front porch and spent her days weeping while listening to a single of Roy Orbison's "Only the Lonely" on her battery-operated record player, a practice, she informed her mother, she planned to continue indefinitely. Ruby, on the other hand, was looking forward to spending time with Suzy, Wendy, and me, and she was pretty sure she'd be able to find a job in camp that would pay her enough to buy the Morris.

Arriving in camp at the beginning of July, it didn't take long for her to find out that there were few job opportunities for her. Franky and Wendy had the oil-barrel-rolling business sewn up, and Suzy and I had a monopoly on bunkhouse bed-making and ashtray-emptying, and we weren't about to bring her in as a partner. "There's only two ways to split twenty dollars," Suzy told her, "so, no dice, kiddo. Go ask the cook. Maybe he'll let you wash dishes."

"You can wash as many dishes as you like," Dave informed her, "but I can only pay you in. . . ." he paused, looking around the cookhouse. "Well, I got this case of empties here," he said, pulling it out from under the sink. "That'll get you fifty cents, and there's more out back."

Individual cases of beer were delivered to Orford Bay by freight boat, complete with handwritten tags stating the customer's name and any pertinent information such as "Harry. One broken bottle—will reimburse next time. Sorry." Most empties were tossed into the bush, but fastidious loggers stacked their cases of empties up against the bunkhouse where wind and rain disintegrated the cardboard, leaving the long-necked bottles in jumbled heaps.

Once Ruby started collecting beer bottles, Suzy, Wendy, and I joined in to help out. "And you don't have to pay us a penny," Suzy reassured her, "but a few bucks wouldn't hurt." The loggers also did their part, kindly handing over their empties right after taking the last sip, though Ernie complained that the second he cracked a beer, Ruby showed up, asking, "Are you finished with that?"

It didn't take long before there were hundreds of bottles stacked on pallets, ready to be loaded onto the freight boat, and this led to speculation about how much money Ruby was going to make. But Mum had the final word. She had bottle-calculating experience, having just completed a tally of the number of bottles of vanilla extract Dave had consumed over the years ("in case he asks for a raise," she explained).

"Well, Dearie," she announced, "I think we're looking at about a hundred and fifty dollars," which was all the encouragement Ruby needed to invite Suzy along on her inaugural drive to the Dairy Queen. She even offered to buy Suzy a Dilly Bar, adding, "You don't have to pay me back, though fifty cents for gas would be nice."

Finally, the big day arrived. The freight boat docked in camp, throwing up a backwash that sent the bottles rattling, but Ruby remained steadfast. She patiently stood by as the camp's food and supplies were dropped onto the float, then it was her turn to instruct the winch operator to lift the pallets of bottles into the ship's hold, but something was wrong. Crew members gathered on deck, pointing at the bottles and shaking their heads, until one of them leaned over the side of the ship and yelled, "We can't take 'em! The breweries don't want them kinda bottles no more! They got the stubbies now, the short ones. Those long-neck ones aren't worth a dime." Timing is everything, and the recent news about changes in the Canadian beer industry had not reached Orford Bay.

Everybody in camp felt bad for Ruby. The loggers threw their empties farther into the bush than before, and Dave, who had not known a sober day for the past several decades, said it was a good thing he didn't drink much beer because he wouldn't want to add to Ruby's sorrow.

However, it was Donna who decisively dealt with the unpleasant situation one afternoon as her father returned home from work.

Carefully lifting "Only the Lonely" off the turntable, she motioned for her father to sit down beside her and offered him some well-needed advice. "You know, Dad," she began in the kindest way possible, "I've been sitting here on this porch, day after day, watching those bottles getting all covered in seagull poop, and it's time you did something about that. Nobody likes to be reminded of things that didn't work out, and I figure Ruby is suffering almost as much as I am."

The next morning the bottles were gone. Uncle Floyd went to work on the boom a little earlier than usual and put his log winch to use relocating them to the deepest part of the bay.

When Ruby returned to Lund at the end of August, she got a job at the Lund Hotel, working in the kitchen, and it was an eye-opening experience. She discovered that tourists were demanding, always asking for flavours of ice cream that were not available, though there was a sign out front with "Strawberry," "Chocolate," and "Vanilla" in big letters, suggesting to anyone asking for "Maple Walnut" that they were out of luck. However, she persevered and made enough money to buy a used Corvair that turned out to be better than the Morris by a long shot, since the headlights worked and she could fit six of her friends in the back and four in the front. And sometimes, when a bunch of them went for a drive, Donna brought along her record player. They put it in the back window and played "Only the Lonely," going slow on the gravel roads so Roy didn't sound as if he were gargling.

Nigel was actually relieved that Ruby hadn't bought the Morris. "It wouldn't have been right to move Gladys and the girls out of the only home they have ever known," he reasoned, "but if you ever need a car battery, remember, the one in the Morris is almost brand new."

Bad Apples

She set out first thing, rowing hard, five miles down the inlet with the baby tied down in the bow and a box of apples sloshing in the water around her ankles.

Just after 9:00 am, Uncle Floyd spotted her rounding the point of Orford Bay. He was on the boom and gave her a cursory wave. "Jesus," he said to himself, "what does she want this time?" Then he leaned into his pike pole and didn't look up again in case she took it as an invitation to row over and have a visit. He wasn't good with small talk at the best of times and never knew what to say to her. She made his heart sink.

From the kitchen window I watched her tie up and start walking up to the house. I shouted to Mum, letting her know that Helga was back again. She had the box of apples under one arm and the baby under the other, probably both soaked through on the bottom, I thought, and as she got closer, some of the apples dropped out through the folds in the cardboard and rolled into the long grass, but Helga didn't stop. There was nothing she could do about it.

At the front door she let out a cheery, "Yoohoo! Anybody home?" and Mum appeared, greeting her the way she always did. "Helga! This is a surprise! And you've brought Juergen with you. Well, come on in. We'll have a cup of coffee."

Helga's visits were always a trial. She was hard to look at, ever since her nose was broken and pushed to one side of her face, but it was really the lack of joy in the young woman's eyes that bothered my mother the most. And there was the smell, something between kerosene and body odour. It hung in the air, and Mum wondered if it was the scent of fear.

She set the cups of coffee on the table, along with two pieces of pie, and Helga settled the baby in the box, using her life jacket as a cushion. "Now, Joan," she announced with enthusiasm. "These apples here are a little tart and you'll have to pick through them for the odd worm, but they'll make real good pies."

"Is Lars away?" Mum asked, referring to Helga's husband.

"Yeah, he's gone fishin' for a few days. Over to Blind Channel for the Chinook run. Says he's gonna make a lot of money, and I can get a couple of yards of fabric for a dress next time we go to Stuart Island."

"That'll be nice," Mum said, settling back, sipping her coffee and waiting for Helga to say why she had really come all this way with another box of her damn apples.

"When I got up this morning," Helga was saying, "I decided to visit my old friend Joan, and I thought Juergen could use a little fresh air. I haven't been out of the house since I hurt my leg. Fell down the stairs." She laughed. "That's me, always somethin', clumsy as an ox." She rattled on: "This pie's real good, Joan. I've always liked lemon meringue, used to eat it all the time, for free." She laughed again. "Can you believe it? That's when I was workin' at The White Lunch, the one on Hastings Street, maybe I told you. Anyhow, I was a dining room waitress. Only the pretty girls got to work in the dining room, and we made real good tips and got to take home the day-old buns." She took a deep breath and started up again. "They gave us a meal every day, too. The egg salad was outta this world." She paused, and Mum knew what was coming; Helga only showed up when she needed a few bucks or a bag of flour, things my mother was more than willing to help out with. She just didn't appreciate the charade.

"Joan, you're not gonna believe it, but you know how I said my leg was hurtin' me?" Helga was telling Mum, drawing her attention back to the present. "Well, in the past few days it's really been actin' up and I wonder if you got some of that iodine?" She lifted her skirt, and Mum took a step back, shocked at the sight of the long gash running down the back of her leg.

"Iodine's not going to help that," she said, trying to maintain an even tone. "You need to see a doctor."

"Just give it to me," Helga snapped, reaching for the bottle. Mom opened her hand and gave it to her, saying, "Okay, Helga, keep it, I don't need it," though she didn't know what she was going to do if one of the loggers came to the door with a bad cut.

Achieving what she had come for, Helga picked up Juergen, popped a bottle of cold milk in his mouth, grabbed the life jacket, and flew out the door, shouting behind her, "You can get at least one pie outta them apples! They're not all bad!"

Uncle Floyd watched her go. The wind had picked up, and he knew it would be tough going once she got out into the inlet. But she could handle the boat, that was for sure, and she was wearing a life jacket, something he never did. Yet he knew that if the boat capsized, the cold would kill her and the baby in a matter of minutes. He'd heard it was like going to sleep, and for a brief moment he felt that might be for the best, then he shook his head in shame and got back to work, stabbing the pike pole deep into a log.

※

THE FIRST TIME I SAW HELGA, FRANKY AND I WERE ON THE float jigging for rock cod. She was sitting on the stern of Lars's fishing boat. They had tied up to the boom while he mended net. We waved to her, and she gave us a smile even though her face looked like Ernie's after he got clipped by the block and tackle.

After about an hour, Lars walked across the boom to bum a cigarette from Uncle Floyd who held out a pack of smokes. Nodding in Helga's direction, we heard him ask, "What happened?"

Lars smiled, as if he were about to tell an amusing story. "We got caught out in bad weather," he answered, taking a cigarette from the pack, "and she fell down the hatch. Clumsy as an ox, that one," he chuckled, throwing up his hands. A beleaguered husband.

Around noon, when Uncle Floyd returned home for lunch, Franky and I were sitting at the kitchen table, waiting for him. We had already told Aunty Patty about Helga "falling down the hatch in a storm," so by the time he sat down to eat, she was irate.

"He's going to kill her one of these days," she fumed, slamming a plate of ham sandwiches down on the table, "and he'll get away with it. Remember when Maisie Madson went missing?" she went on. "Her husband told the RCMP she fell out of the boat and sank like a stone. I bet she did! And there was that other one, I can't remember her name, but she had the twins."

"Oh, that was Edith Whitlock," Uncle Floyd answered.

"Yeah, that's right. They said she took the boat out and never returned," Aunty Patty scoffed, "but I heard from Charlie that when the police went to the house a week later, the bread was still in the oven, and any damn fool knows a woman won't go out if she's got bread in the oven."

Franky and I remained silent, continuing to listen to the adults talk—well, mostly Aunty Patty. However, when Uncle Floyd lit a cigarette and leaned back in his chair, we knew he was ready to say something.

"I've known Lars since he was married to his first wife, Elaine, so we go back a long time," he said, taking a drag on his cigarette. "He beat the bejesus out of her. She was in and out of hospital in Campbell River all the time getting patched up. The doctors called her a 'regular' until one of them told her that the next time she came in, she might be in a canvas bag, you know, the ones they use to ship dead loggers outta camps."

Franky and I were barely breathing as he went on, describing how Elaine returned home and got ready for the next time her husband became violent, and "she let him have it with a gunshot to the knee."

"That's right," Aunty Patty agreed, "but only because the rifle was heavy; otherwise Elaine would have lifted it a little higher and shot him where he most deserved it."

"Ever since," Uncle Floyd continued, "Lars has walked with a limp and whenever he goes to Stuart Island, Charlie Joe asks him how the hell he ended up with 'that haywire leg,' as if he's forgotten, but ol' Charlie never forgets anything."

Looking out the window at the fishing boat, Franky nudged me, "Should I get the .22?" he whispered, "I could nail him in the other knee, easy."

—﹨❘⁄—

BY LATE AUGUST, THE BOOM WAS READY TO GO TO VANCOUVER. Uncle Floyd and Ernie were on the float waiting for the scaler to arrive, but the plane was late, and they took shelter from the wind, ducking into the boat shed.

"I hope they didn't send the guy who carries his boots around in that little suitcase," Uncle Floyd said with disdain. "He scaled the boom last time and I figure he was off by a couple hundred board feet."

"Oh, that guy," Ernie said, taking a cigarette from behind his ear and lighting it. "I saw him at Stuart Island last week when I went to pick up the boom chains. I know what you mean, those guys with the big educations always think they're right."

"I also ran into that sonofabitch Lars. He tried to bum five bucks off me and I told him to get lost." Ernie paused. "You heard about his wife, eh? What's her name?"

"Helga," answered Uncle Floyd. "What did he do to her this time?"

"Well," Ernie hesitated, "they're sayin' she drowned. Ol' Charlie was sittin' on the dock there, and after Lars buggered off, he calls me over and says the RCMP went to the camp to take a look around and her life jacket was still hangin' on the dock, but that young guy, Corporal Stewart, said they couldn't charge him because there wasn't any evidence."

—√ı⁄—

THAT NIGHT, THE ADULTS WERE SITTING AROUND THE KITCHEN table, and nobody was talking. Suzy, Wendy, and I huddled together on the sofa quietly playing Clue. We were about to discover who the murderer was, though it was fairly obvious. Mum poured coffee and pushed the can of milk towards Aunty Patty. Dad got up and threw some wood in the stove, and Uncle Floyd lit a cigarette, letting the wick in the lamp burn a little lower before speaking.

"I was best man at Lars's first wedding," he said, "when he married Elaine. She was from Squirrel Cove, but she went to town for a few years and was workin' at that White Lunch on Hastings Street. The place with the real good pie. I guess that's where he met both of them."

I got up to call Smokey in for the night, and as he settled himself in a corner of the the kitchen, Uncle Floyd broke the silence for the second time, saying, "You, know, if that sonofabitch comes around here again, I'm gonna wrap a boom chain around his ankles and drop him into the chuck."

"Well, you'd get away with it," Aunty Patty commented. "People around here drown all the time."

Chapter Ten

Calling It Quits

The anticipatory pleasure of free cheese and crackers, Canadian pastimes, and how "Surprise!" is never a good word.

Logging the Matterhorn

THE DAY UNCLE KURT FELL FLAT ON HIS BACK IN THE MUD, HE
wasn't hurt, but he didn't move for some time. He lay there, staring up
into the black clouds overhead as the rain pounded down, smacking
him in the face and drenching any remaining part of his body that
was not encased in mud. He was wondering if Willcock & Wankel was
done for this time. And he was also wondering how he was going to
break it to my father that the company's biggest asset had just slipped
over a precipice and was laying in two hundred feet of water at the
bottom of the inlet.

Before Uncle Kurt landed in the mud, he and my father had been
making some decent money for the first time. They had four trucks
hauling logs every day, all day, and a crew of ten men. This was the
measure of their success. But since they were working in a rainforest
that gets over two hundred days of rain a year—and the rest of the
time it's overcast and just getting ready to rain again—logging trucks
often slid off the road, and when that happened, there were flat tires to
repair. I suppose that after Uncle Kurt and Dad had each changed a few
hundred truck tires while up to their eyeballs in mud, they decided it
was time to find an easier way to transport logs. This was an especially
pertinent decision when, in 1965, they got a timber licence on a mountainside they referred to as "The Matterhorn," because it was incredibly
steep. Too steep for trucks.

The latest innovations in logging equipment could be found at the annual Truck Loggers' Convention, which took place at the Bayshore Inn, a swishy hotel on Vancouver's waterfront. For the logging community, this convention was a big deal. Loggers pulled their suits out of mothballs and showed up at the hotel to act like big shots for a few days of what is now known as "networking" but used to be called "business and a few drinks."

In the parking lot of the hotel, all the latest logging equipment was on display. The newfangled machinery spoke to loggers of easier days in the woods where a flip of a switch could lift logs into the air, and before you clicked your heels three times, the logs were in the water and on their way to Vancouver to be sold. Sometimes Dad took Wendy and me to the convention, and we were always amazed to see the equipment parked out in front of the hotel. It was uniformly bright yellow and sparkling clean, nothing at all like the machinery in camp.

At the convention, loggers were invited up to hospitality suites where salesmen plied them with drinks while singing the praises of the yellow beauties in the parking lot. And that is how, after a lot of hoopla and handshakes, and a $180,000 bank loan, Dad and Uncle Kurt ended up with the Vagner, a piece of machinery manufactured specifically to haul logs on steep inclines. It resembled a praying mantis right down to the "arms" that were designed to lift up one end of a bundle of logs and drag the load downhill. Lickedy split.

At the foot of The Matterhorn, the log dump plunged seventy-five feet straight down into the ocean. The sheer drop was shored up by a row of upright logs, and from far out in the inlet, it looked like the wall of a fortress. The Vagner would pull up near the edge of the log dump. Then the logs were unhooked and pushed over the edge, crashing into the water like a bomb going off. It was a dangerous job but big on thrills.

However, the Vagner was trouble from the get-go, and Dad and Uncle Kurt talked about it as if it were an ailing relative: the Vagner was overheating, acting up, breaking down, stalling, grinding, leaking this, leaking that. There was no end to the trouble.

When machinery broke down, the first thing to do was to get on the radio telephone and call Finlay's Caterpillar Co. for help. This company sold and serviced most of the logging equipment on the coast, and whenever there was a problem with the Vagner, they always had an answer: "Yes, the engine part will be on the next freight boat." "Yes, the mechanic can fly in to camp, but he says it will take three days to do the repairs so you'll have to find a bed for him." "Yes, we'll have a plane in there tomorrow to pick up the part. Just make sure it's not too heavy or the pilot can't take off." Or: "You need a barge to move that? We'll have one there early next week." Dad said that he wished he worked for Finlay's and every logging show had a Vagner; then he could retire.

It was raining to beat hell the day the Vagner went over the log dump. When Uncle Kurt pulled up with the last load of logs for the day, water was pouring over the dump in torrents of mud and debris. He was just about to unhook the logs when the Vagner shifted in the mud, not much, but enough to slide one log over the edge. Then all hell broke loose; in a matter of seconds the remainder of the logs tumbled over the precipice, yanking the Vagner onto its side and dragging it over the dump in a cacophony of crashing metal and splintering wood.

Seconds later, Uncle Kurt was laying on his back in a sea of mud. It was a miracle he got out of the Vagner before it went over. All he could remember was looking out the cab door straight down at the water and the next thing he knew he was on the ground. Coming to his senses, he knew he had to get back to camp and call Finlay's; they would know what to do. After that, he would call Dad who was in Vancouver at the time reassuring their bankers that Willcock & Wankel Logging Ltd. was doing so well they wanted to borrow more money.

When the call came, I heard Dad pick up the phone and say, "How's it goin?" Then his tone changed. "Oh jeez, is that right, eh? It was raining to beat hell? Slippery, eh. . . ? The logs pulled 'er over. . . ? How long did Finlay's say it would be until they could get a crane in there to pull 'er up. . . ? Jesus. I'll be back in camp tomorrow."

The Vagner was pulled out of the saltchuck and sold for peanuts, and somehow my father and uncle finagled another bank loan, bought

Whaddaya Know

GROWING UP AROUND LOGGERS, I BELIEVED THAT INJURIES WERE just part of the job. Uncle Harold managed with only eight fingers, and a guy called Russell put a sock in the end of one boot to make up for a couple of missing toes. When Uncle Harry's leg was shattered by a log, everyone marvelled at how he "got around on those crutches." However, his leg never really healed, and for years he was the one on crutches in all the family photos. He even got married on crutches and, afterwards, became a farmer and herded dairy cows on his crutches. He'd wave one crutch in the air while yelling at the cows to get a move on, then he'd chase after them, his crutches swinging out in front of his legs as he raced across the fields. He never complained.

In our family, we thought Dad was one of the lucky ones, not like the other guys whose badly-set bones and phantom limbs ached on cold winter nights. He made a complete recovery after getting hit in the back by a log and cracking several vertebrae. His only other work-related injury was that he was a little hard of hearing, but it was nothing to worry about and only to be expected in his line of work. However, his hearing worsened, year by year, and by the time he was in his mid-fifties, he was almost deaf.

Each day, from the moment he began work until lights out, the thunderous cacophony of machinery never stopped: power saws screamed, donkey engines roared, horns and whistles blasted. Even turning the damn lights out at night was ear-splitting, as the camp's generator roared so loudly that fishermen out in the inlet could hear it. If an engine on any piece of equipment needed fixing, it was Dad who had his head under the hood while another logger revved the motor a hundred times over. Ear plugs? Ear muffs? Forget about it. In the sixties, there wasn't much awareness about work-related hearing loss.

Besides, my father hadn't realized how bad his hearing loss was until he got a nudge from an unbiased source.

There was an old prospector's cabin about a mile back in the Orford Valley where dynamite was kept. That was the law. Explosives had to be far away from human settlement and under lock and key. Whenever the crew was building road, Dad hiked to the "powder shack" to get some dynamite, the most efficient tool for blasting a road through virgin forests, and he always carried a rifle slung over one shoulder, just in case. For the most part, the wolves in the valley avoided human contact, but the grizzlies were another story. They could be aggressive, especially in the fall.

Arriving at the powder shack early one October morning, Dad was fiddling with the rusty lock on the door when he felt something brush against his back. At first, he thought it was just the rifle strap slipping off his shoulder but then it happened again, the slightest brush, soft but firm, and he slowly turned around and came face to face with a curious young grizzly. Afterwards, he couldn't remember how he got onto the roof of the cabin, but he found himself up there looking down at the bear. He fired off a few shots to frighten it, and it took off into the bush. Dad remained on the roof for some time, trembling, not so much over the encounter with the bear, but more over the fact that he hadn't heard the big animal snuffling up behind him.

The solution was to buy a hearing aid. The one he got was big and clumsy, with wires running from an earpiece to a microphone the size of a pack of smokes. It also had a dial that increased the volume but didn't improve the quality of the sound. It was like choosing between a crypt-like silence or the Stanley Cup playoffs, and nothing in between. When new types of hearing aids became available, Dad tried them out, one after another, but none of them improved his hearing or were less awkward to use than the previous ones. Once he even got a hearing aid concealed inside a pair of eyeglasses, but the frames were thick and heavy and made him look like a mob boss.

Eventually, he stopped wearing hearing aids altogether. He'd leave them on a dresser in the bedroom where I would pick one up and stick it in my ear to hear sounds amplified but hollow and echoey, as if I were at the bottom of a well.

Dad became socially awkward and, frankly, an embarrassment to me and my sisters. When we had friends over, he would walk away in the middle of a conversation, or he'd change the subject so abruptly that everyone looked at each other in surprise. Family members spoke to him in booming voices and sometimes I even wrote him notes to clarify a point. I also got in the habit of shouting at every man who was around the same age as my father, toning it down only when I was reminded by more than one man who grumbled, "I'm not deaf, you know."

As his hearing worsened, he stopped going to church, saying it didn't really matter because he'd heard all the sermons before, and, secretly, I was relieved since he was always a line behind or ahead when saying prayers or singing hymns, and other churchgoers gave him funny looks. Restaurants were the worst, with clattering dishes, background music, and everyone talking at once. He couldn't distinguish one sound from another. Parties weren't much better. It was impossible for him to figure out what the hell people were saying by lip-reading or following gestures and facial expressions. But he tried his best by telling jokes; he talked, and others listened and laughed. If someone spoke to him, he usually answered by saying, "Isn't that something," or "Whaddaya know," which often hit the mark, or close to it.

He retreated onto the golf course and into the solitude of our basement, where he spent hours carving birds, small canoes, and totems. This was where he was happiest. By the time he was in his seventies, he was no longer ashamed of being deaf and could cope in any social situation. "After all," he said, "most people like to talk about themselves. So, I just ask a few questions, they talk, I smile, and everybody's happy."

Of Little Consequence

AS A RULE, BUSH PLANES FLEW INTO CAMPS FIRST THING IN THE morning to deliver mechanics and machinery or arrived late in the afternoon to bring loggers back to work. The drone of a Beaver coming up the inlet at any other time brought all activity in Orford Bay to a standstill. The cook came outside and stood on the boardwalk, floury hands on hips, his face turned skyward, and Mum appeared on our front porch, broom in one hand, the other shading her eyes as she watched the plane go by. On the beach, Franky and Wendy and I stopped playing and whispered to each other that the Beaver was headed up the inlet to Uncle Harold's camp, not wanting to say out loud what we all knew—another logger had been killed.

Uncle Harold's methods had not improved with age. In the 1960s, he was still running his logging show with complete disregard for the safety of his crew. He continued to get away with it, too, even though dead loggers were shipped out of his camp with the same regularity some people take out their garbage.

Picking up dead men wore down the bush pilots, and they would sometimes land in Orford Bay for a cup of coffee and a reinforcing piece of pie before continuing up the inlet, where stone-faced loggers waited to lift a corpse into the plane. The bodies were laid in the aisle with the feet extending right into the cockpit, and when a Beaver ran into turbulence, the boots rocked back and forth, tapping against the pilot's seat. One pilot told Mum about the time he flew a body out of Uncle Harold's camp on a blustery day; the plane hit an air pocket, and the corpse lurched into a sitting position as the pilot turned and met the dead man eye to eye.

Nobody in Orford Bay ever mentioned Uncle Harold by name or talked about how many loggers got killed working for him—it had been going on too long, and it seemed as if there would never be an end to it.

We had to put up with him at Christmas, however. He'd show up with a cheap ham and an expensive bottle of Scotch, and everyone would be polite, even when he took his half-empty bottle of booze home at the end of the night.

He never found Jesus or a conscience but he made a lot of money. Then one day he dropped dead in Woodward's department store, keeled over at a checkout on the food floor, clutching a bag of frozen peas. His children were left with a fortune, which they fought over in court for years, making their lawyers plenty rich.

Good Grief

EVERY MORNING, AFTER THE LOGGERS HAD LEFT FOR WORK, Suzy and I went to the bunkhouse to sweep the floor, make the beds, and empty the ashtrays. It only took a few hours to get everything done. After that, we were supposed to leave, no snooping around, but we often stayed to read the loggers' magazines and, on occasion, their personal letters, something we weren't proud of. But it was unavoidable since the guys left them lying around. And the only thing we learned was that men thought their wives would be interested in a couple of pages about how to change a tire in the rain or the cost of new boots. So, for the most part I stuck with *Reader's Digest* and Suzy read *True Detective* magazines. "They're just like *Nancy Drews*," she enthused, "except strippers and waitresses get murdered instead of old ladies."

We usually sat on Mike's bed, our backs against the wall, feet hanging over the side, with a stack of magazines between us. He was tidy, and unlike the other guys who hung their stinking work clothes and rain gear next to their beds, he had a three-piece suit hanging on the wall. It was comfy sitting there, leaning into the soft wool of the jacket.

I sometimes wondered why a guy who never left camp would have a nice suit like that. One morning, sitting on the bed with Suzy, I asked her what she thought about it, but she was engrossed in a *True*

Detective and gave me one of her absentminded replies. "I don't know," she said, turning a page. "I guess he's saving it for a special occasion."

Mike first came to Orford Bay as a winter watchman. After camp shut down and the crew flew out, he was left to keep an eye on the logging equipment. He loved the isolation of camp because he was a loner. There were lots of guys like that. They didn't have homes, and if anybody asked about their personal lives, the stories were vague and ran along the lines of having a sister up north or an ex-wife back east, they weren't exactly sure, they'd lost touch. However, nobody asked Mike much about himself. It was understood that he was a guy who kept to himself.

Lingering in the bunkhouse one day after Suzy had left, I settled in to read a *True Detective*, figuring I'd take my sister's advice and give one a try. The story I chose was about a blonde from Kentucky who ended up in a ditch with her stockings around her neck. The *True Detectives* had few clues to go on until a short order cook at Jimmy's Diner, where the dead woman had worked, was overheard saying, "She was a real nice gal, but a little too friendly with some of the customers, if ya know what I mean." I didn't know what he meant. I had to keep reading.

Coming to the end of the story, it had not been made clear how being "too friendly" resulted in murder, but I was satisfied to find out that "the loner at the end of the bar" was the murderer—the guy with no friends or family, so it didn't matter that he got sent to the electric chair. Nobody was going to miss him.

Returning the magazine to the stack beside the bed, I stood up and turned round to smooth out the blanket when I saw that Mike's suit was askew, almost falling off the hanger. Reaching up to adjust it I noticed the name on the label: Modernize Tailors, 5 West Pender Street, and remembered Mum pointing out the location when we drove past on our way to the Ho Ho restaurant.

Before coming to Orford Bay, Mike worked for other logging companies on the coast and spent his winters in a hotel room on Vancouver's Downtown Eastside. That's where he found Smokey in a box on the street with his brothers and sister, two bucks each, take your pick. Around that time, he must also have heard about Modernize Tailors. It was just a few blocks over in Chinatown, and I imagined him going there to get measured, choose fabric, and order his tailcoat jacket, pinstripe trousers, and vest.

Along with being an excellent rigging slinger, Mike was the first-aid attendant in camp. He had experience with that kind of thing after being a medic in Italy during the War. Like everything else he did, he was quiet and calm no matter what and he made injured loggers feel that they were going to be okay. When Andy's chainsaw bucked back, ripping into his leg from knee to crotch, Mike scrambled through the contents of the first-aid kit for a bandage big enough to close the wound that lay open like a book. Coming up empty-handed, he took off his shirt and wrapped it around the thigh, tying the sleeves like a tourniquet, then securing the leg with baling wire. Later that night, after Andy had been flown out to hospital, Mike came over to our house to get another shirt from the commissary. He didn't say anything about what had happened that day; he just got the shirt and left.

That fall, back in North Vancouver, Mum turned on the radio one morning and heard that a man had been injured in a logging accident in Orford Bay. The name of the victim was not given. She immediately called the RCMP in Campbell River and was told the crew in Orford Bay were prohibited from talking to anyone until the police investigation was complete, and no, they couldn't tell her the name of the logger who had been hurt; she just had to wait along with everyone else.

For the next five days my mother ran the names of the crew around in her head, over and over, thinking about the jobs they did and which were the most dangerous and who was overly confident, who was a little careless. At the same time, she tried not to think about Dad being the one who was hurt but she couldn't stop herself, and the only consolation she had was that Mike was there and he would have known what to do.

When the call came, it was Dad on the other end of the line, and Mum was so relieved to hear his voice that, at first, it didn't register with her when he said that Mike had been killed. "No, that's not right," she replied. "The police said 'injured,' nothing about anybody getting killed."

"A coroner had to declare him," Dad answered, keenly aware his words were being broadcast up and down the coast via the radio telephone. "Prior to that, we had to report it as an injury."

Mum broke the news to me and Suzy and Wendy when we got home from school. Later that night, lying in bed, I tried to make sense of it, telling myself that perhaps life was fair after all since the guy with no friends or family was the one who got killed. But it didn't feel right to think about Mike that way. I just felt sad.

The day Mike died, "everything was goin' real good," Dad recounted, several months after the accident, as if he were still trying to understand it himself. "Then a log got loose and took off down a steep slope," he said, holding his hand at a forty-five-degree angle to illustrate. "Mike saw it comin' and dove under a fallen tree to get the hell out of the way."

My father went on to explain how everything stopped, and the crew stood at the top of the hillside, scanning the landscape, waiting for Mike to appear and wave a hand so they could get back to work. After a few minutes, Dad headed downhill. The only sounds on the mountain were his caulk boots scraping over boulders and crunching into wood as he jumped from stump to stump, stopping every few seconds to listen for Mike's call. When he did find him tucked under the tree, he looked peaceful, like he was going to be okay. Maybe just knocked out. He only had a small mark on his head and the skin wasn't even broken. Dad took a vial of smelling salts out of his pocket, cracked it open and put it under Mike's nose. Nothing. Then, he listened to his chest. Nothing. After that, he started mouth-to-mouth but, in his words, "I called it quits after an hour."

Mike was laid across the back seat of the crummy, taken back to camp, and flown out to Campbell River later that afternoon. Smokey crawled under his bed and wouldn't come out.

The following week, the loggers chipped in and ordered a flight to Vancouver to attend the funeral. The cook was the only one to stay behind, and he drank his sorrow away.

"Do you think they put him in his suit?" I asked Suzy. We were reading on her bed, legs against the wall, feet hanging over. "What do you mean?" she asked, distractedly turning a page of her book. "For the funeral," I said, "do you think he was wearing his suit?" She stopped reading and looked up, actually giving some thought to what I had asked. "Oh, yeah, I would say so," she replied. "It was a special occasion, right?"

Huladay

FOLLOWING AN UNUSUALLY SUCCESSFUL LOGGING SEASON IN the mid-sixties, my parents decided to take their first international holiday. The vacation promised to be nothing like our family's annual camping trip. Every year we found ourselves huddled in a tent waiting for the rain to let up so we could partake in the quintessential Canadian pastime of swimming in a hypothermia-inducing lake while insisting, "It's not that bad once you get used to it."

In stark contrast, Mum and Dad were going to Hawaii to frolic in ocean water that was so warm, my mother claimed, you could just walk out of the sea and flop down on the sand; there was no need to warm up around a campfire. And if you got too hot basking under the tropical sun, you could sip on drinks called "My Ties," which according to Mum was Hawaiian for "drink with an umbrella"—go figure.

However, my mother was learning more than how to order a drink in Hawaiian. She had bought a phrase book in order to "communicate with the locals." Dinner at our house was no longer dinner, it was a "luau," dresses were "muumuus," and apparently "aloha" could mean hello and goodbye, which explained why so many people who went to Hawaii said they had a hard time leaving. Mum's fluency in the Hawaiian language also gave her the confidence to make "bilingual" jokes. She must have told everyone she knew (several times over) that she and Dad were going on a "huladay." Then she explained herself:

"We're going to Hawaii! Get it? Hula dancing?" and she'd bust a few hula moves for the slow learners.

She had booked passage to Hawaii on a swishy cruise ship called the *S.S. Gloriana*. These were the last days of dignified international travel, not like today where you have to take off half your clothes and get groped, and swabbed, and x-rayed, before cramming yourself into a seat designed for people who are not tall enough to ride roller coasters. But I digress. In the sixties, cruise ship passengers were allowed to have friends and family come aboard for a few hours to say their goodbyes in staterooms replete with flower arrangements and bottles of champagne. Travelling was a big deal.

When "Bon Voyage" day arrived, Suzy, Wendy and I put on our church coats, hats, and white gloves and accompanied Mum and Dad in a taxi to the Vancouver docks where the *Gloriana* was tied up. Uncle Kurt and Dotty were also there to wish them a great trip as well, which was so kind, since they were officially separated and unofficially hated each other. The plan was that they would give us girls a ride home afterwards.

My parents were beyond excited to be going on such a ritzy holiday and proudly showed off their stateroom with its bunk beds, dollhouse-size bathroom, and single porthole (the staterooms with flowers and champagne were on the upper decks). Our family squished together along the lower bunk while Uncle Kurt and Dotty took up chairs opposite. The adults drank Scotch in paper cups, poured from a mickey Uncle Kurt kept in his back pocket, he explained, for "emergencies or when I want a drink," and we all chatted and laughed and snacked on tiny sandwiches held together with toothpick flags of the *S.S. Gloriana*.

After several Scotches, Dotty performed the hula for us, dancing around the stateroom expertly swaying her hips and waving her hands around exactly like the Hawaiian dancers on the TV show Mum had made us watch. In fact, Dotty was so adept at the hula it seemed to me that she must have been practicing—a lot.

When we heard the "All ashore that's going ashore" announcement, Suzy handed Wendy and me our coats and gloves, we kissed Mum and Dad, and waited for Uncle Kurt and Dotty to say their goodbyes, but they didn't budge. Dotty asked for another Scotch, and Uncle Kurt lit a cigarette and settled back in his chair. Outside the stateroom, other visitors were saying their last goodbyes, while a ship's steward marched up and down the corridor, ringing a bell over and over and reciting the "all ashore" announcement in an increasingly stern tone of voice. But inside the stateroom, nobody moved, and I leaned over to look under the bunk bed, imagining my sisters and I stowed away there for a week eating tiny stale sandwiches.

Tension in the stateroom increased. Uncomfortable silences stretched between repeated polite encouragements from Mum and Dad for Uncle Kurt and Dotty to accompany us girls off the ship. Still, nobody moved. Uncle Kurt was blowing smoke rings and Dotty seemed to doze off. The sounds of sailors shouting to each other as they loosened the ship's moorings floated in through the porthole. A few more minutes ticked by, and the steward was shouting, "Final call! All ashore that's going ashore. Final call!" Mum gave Suzy the nod and she grabbed Wendy and me by the hand, and we pounded up several flights of stairs to the main deck and raced down the gangplank just as the ship's whistle blew, announcing its imminent departure.

It was probably at the precise moment my sisters and I landed on the dock, sweaty and out-of-breath, that Uncle Kurt and Dotty roused themselves, looked conspiratorially at each other, and burst forth with "Surrrpriiiiise! We're coming with you!" at which point Dad spewed Scotch and bits of egg sandwich on the wall opposite him while Mum sat frozen, not knowing the Hawaiian phrase for "what the f**k." Then the *Gloriana's* whistle blew for the last time, and she slipped her moorings and sailed out of Vancouver Harbour.

My sisters and I caught a bus home, and I phoned Franky the minute we got in the door to tell him his parents were on their way to Hawaii, but he smugly informed me that he already knew about their trip and had kept the secret because he was the kind of person you could trust not to tell stuff you were not supposed to tell. My sisters and I agreed that his mother had probably threatened to wring his neck if he said anything.

On board the *Gloriana*, Dotty and Uncle Kurt retired to their stateroom (on an upper deck), and my parents remained in their stateroom surrounded by the debris of the bon voyage party: empty bottles, full ashtrays, and sad little flags of the *Gloriana* with bent toothpick flagpoles. They were stunned. For over fifteen years, they had put up with the crazy antics of Uncle Kurt and Dotty and now they were about to share the holiday of their lives with them. What had just happened?

Later that night, in the ship's bar, Uncle Kurt explained to Dad that he and Dotty wanted to "give 'er another try," and they had thought that taking a vacation with my parents was just what they needed, which seemed to be the case—at first. As the *Gloriana* chugged towards Hawaii, the reunited lovebirds danced the nights away, but nobody had a clue that Dotty was just warming up.

Docking in Honolulu, she quickstepped down the gangplank and into a series of bars overflowing with American sailors, and luckily for them, she was just the gal to liven up any place with her Arthur Murray School of Dance prowess and the ability to drink any one of them under the table. Uncle Kurt spent his days trying to track her down, without success, and my parents spent too much of their precious holiday time consoling him.

Not long after getting back from Hawaii, Uncle Kurt and Dotty filed for divorce. He blamed the "huladay" for the breakup of the marriage, telling Dad, "We never should have agreed to go along with you and Joan on that trip. Dotty and I needed to be alone."

MOLLS AND CANNONBALLS

ONCE IN YOUR LIFETIME, IF YOU'RE LUCKY, THE STARS WILL
align, and you'll get the big cosmic bonus you've always dreamed of.
For Dad and Uncle Kurt, their years of constantly living one breakdown away from going belly-up came to an end in 1968 when they sold
Willcock & Wankel Logging Ltd. to a large forest corporation. Timing
is everything, and they got that right, selling out at the height of the
timber market. It was a miracle. With over seventy years of logging
experience between them, my father and uncle had spent much of that
time slogging through mud, dealing with lousy equipment, and, more
often than not, separated from their families. But all their hard work
had finally paid off. They signed on the dotted line, shook hands, and
each went his own way. It was time to begin new lives.

With his jackpot, Dad promptly retired, paid off the mortgage, and
installed a swimming pool in the backyard, (which he decided not to
heat because "it's not that bad once you get used to it"). Uncle Kurt,
on the other hand, got himself a racehorse and a Lincoln Continental,
and it turned out the Lincoln ran better than the horse. After that,
he doubled down and bought his way into the good graces of some
bad guys who hung out at Vancouver's horse track. At first, there were
handshakes and backslaps galore, steak dinners, pretty women, and
promises of lots of money.

However, one hot August afternoon when he arrived at our house in North Vancouver with two of his new best friends, he seemed nervous—and maybe even a little scared. He knew Mum and Dad were away for the weekend and he thought he could spend the afternoon sitting around the pool with his friends, but after docking the freighter-size Lincoln in our driveway, he was taken aback when Suzy, Wendy, and I ran out to greet him. He hadn't counted on Mum and Dad leaving us alone for the weekend, and we certainly hadn't expected him to drop by unannounced. But here he was, with a short, skinny guy named Jackie and a young woman with a hairdo the size and density of an astronaut's helmet. She was Jackie's girlfriend, and he called her "Babydoll" and "Sweetheart," but not in a nice way, more like he was calling a dog. Meanwhile, Uncle Kurt kept smiling and laughing like a game show host every time Jackie uttered a few words.

Breezing past us, they made themselves right at home, and in no time at all, they were lounging in deck chairs around the pool. Jackie snapped open a small briefcase to reveal a portable mini-bar, and he began making martinis. This was so "Frank Sinatra." Who was this guy? Uncle Kurt continued fawning all over him and dutifully made several trips inside the house for ice and cocktail napkins, and anything else his new friend demanded, including suntan lotion, towels, and roast beef sandwiches—*our* suntan lotion, *our* towels, and *our* roast beef.

As the afternoon wore on, our guests got tipsy, then drunk, and tossed olive pits and cigarette butts into the pool. Then things got ugly. Wendy and I were fooling around in the shallow end, splashing each other close to where the adults were sitting when Jackie suddenly erupted, "Hey, hey, hey! Willya stop your splashin' and makin' such a goddamn racket! Your uncle and I are talkin' business here! Scram!" Then, he turned to "Babydoll-Sweetheart" and said, "You can get lost, too. Go swimmin' or sumpin," and she slunk off into the shallow end of the pool, careful not to get her hair wet. The violence in this guy's voice was palpable. Wendy and I were stunned, and Suzy had even looked up from her book to see what was going on. She motioned us over to where she was sitting—and it didn't take long for us to formulate a plan of attack.

Wendy did the first cannonball, landing in the pool with a splash worthy of a baby orca, and Suzy and I were right behind her, sending a wall of water over top of Jackie and Uncle Kurt as they scrambled to escape, knocking over the mini-bar and overturning deck chairs. But there was no way out, because somebody had locked the pool gate from the outside. The Willcock girls were taking no prisoners.

Meanwhile, "Babydoll-Sweetheart" was caught in the crossfire. Her astronaut hair was dripping wet and had decompressed. Apparently, this kind of thing can make a woman angry and scream at men about why the #@&* they brought her to a house with a #@&*ing swimming pool and horrible #@&*ing teenagers. The men will not like having vodka bottles thrown in their direction and they will leap over a locked gate, run to their car, and peel out of the driveway, leaving the woman to take a taxi home. Before she can do that, however, she will demand a hairdryer and a can of hairspray, so the taxi driver will not be able to judge her based on what appears to be a dead mongoose plastered to her skull.

A few days later, two plainclothes policemen knocked on our door. They had lots of questions for Mum and Dad and produced photos of dead guys, including a few with bullet holes in their foreheads. My parents were asked if they recognized any of the men, which they didn't, even though Mum thought one very surprised-looking guy, with a hole right between his eyes, resembled our dentist. The police went on to explain that Jackie was not just a gangster but the most powerful and violent mobster in Vancouver. Of course, this news shook up my parents, though the police assured them Jackie had no reason to go after *our* family—except, I thought, he might have been a little put off by our poolside hospitality—something my sisters and I never bothered to mention.

Luckily, not long afterwards, Jackie was arrested, and I forgot about him for the most part until I was going to university and got a summer job with a law firm in Vancouver. One night, when everyone in the office was having a few beers after work, a senior lawyer started talking about a trial in the mid-sixties of a local crime boss. He said that at that time he and all the other prosecutors on the case had twenty-four-hour police protection. The trial had been conducted behind bulletproof glass, a precedent-setting safety precaution in Vancouver courts. He went on to say that he lived in fear of the mobster coming after him, no matter what the verdict, because this was a criminal who always took revenge—even for the slightest insult.

When he mentioned the mobster's name, I wasn't really surprised that he had been talking about Jackie. However, I was more grateful than ever that Jackie had been imprisoned. You see, I had never admitted to anyone, not even to myself, that I had worried about him coming back to our house and shooting me and my sisters in the forehead, and that maybe I would have ended up in one of the police photos, with someone I didn't know saying I resembled their dentist.

Back Home

IT WAS A RAINY AFTERNOON IN ORFORD BAY, NOTHING UNUSUAL about that. The clouds hung low over the bay, and the rain came down, hitting the surface of the water in a million pinpricks. It was the perfect day for Wendy, Franky, and me to go fishing for rock cod off the log float at the mouth of the bay. We weren't going to stay too long; rock cod are easy to catch, but as the cook had reminded us that morning, they are hard to eat since they're more bones than meat. He also said he never wanted us to bring him another rock cod for as long as he lived.

In any case, the cook's words did not curb our enthusiasm. We went jigging, and as expected, it didn't take long before we were all reeling in cod, careful not to pull them up so fast that their eyes bugged out of their heads, which is what we used to do for a laugh before one of the loggers asked us how we would like to have eyes the size of golf balls. After that, we stopped. None of us wanted golf ball eyes.

We cleaned the fish, threw the guts into the saltchuck, and were packing up to go home when Wendy said, "Do you hear that?" And sure enough, the "putt, putt, putt" of a motorboat grew louder, and a few minutes later, a small, open boat came around the point. There was one guy at the helm gripping the tiller of the outboard motor with two hands, pushing it back and forth like he was scrubbing a floor, while another guy sat in the middle seat clutching the gunwales. They looked miserable, hunched over against the wind and rain, wearing oilskins that were too big. We stood watching them, dumbfounded. Nobody who lived on the coast would go out in weather like this in an open boat. These guys were probably from the city. The boat headed straight for the float, bow first, and came to a crashing halt before the motor was shut off. Yep, city guys for sure.

They stared at us; we stared back. The wind blew, the rain came down, and finally one of them introduced himself, not by giving his name, but by saying he was from some big university that we had probably heard of, but we hadn't. After that, he got down to business and asked if we knew about any "Indian" burial sites in Orford Bay, and on cue, without any hesitation at all, we each answered with a resounding "Nope." But of course, we were lying.

By then, the rain was blowing into the bay sideways, but Wendy, Franky, and I held steady, smiling our best school-photo smiles while the men in the boat conferred with each other and tried to read a wet map that was flapping in the wind. Then, the guy at the tiller asked if we knew where the Orford River was. Franky took that one. "The funny thing is," he said, "even though this is Orford Bay and you might *think* we would have an Orford River here, we don't. That river over by the cliffs is called the Bazooka River. It should be right there on your map. The Orford River is about three miles down the inlet. So, you gotta go back the way you came. Just look for the camp there, and the river is right after that. You can't miss it." After more map-flapping, I figured it was time to offer our visitors a rock cod, and just like that, they got busy turning the boat around and "putt, putted" out of the bay. We never saw them again.

Afterwards, Mum gave our lie her stamp of approval with the comment, "darn right," which was what she said when she emphatically agreed with something. She also added, "If they found anything, they'd probably haul it all back to Vancouver and put it behind glass!" Then she paused, pointedly looking at the rock cod hanging from our fishy fingers, and said, "I am not cooking that fish, give it to Aunty Patty. I got it last time."

When the sun came out later that afternoon, I ran over to the Orford River with Franky and Wendy to play on the sandbars, glancing up every now and then to the cliffs on the opposite side of the river. The summer before, Mum and Dad had taken a speedboat over to the mouth of the river to do some fishing. They had probably just wanted to get away from camp and kids for a while because neither of them liked to fish, especially my father who was definitely not patient when it came to waiting for a salmon to show interest in a chunk of bacon on a hook.

Dad's attention was elsewhere. He was looking up at the cliffs towering over the river, when he saw the markings on the rock face. That's just the way it was with him; he noticed things, old things.

Walking across the beach with the crew, caulk boots squelching through piles of seaweed, something would catch his eye: an unusual shape or a deliberate difference in the contours of a stone, evidence of human hands at work. Once, glancing down, he spotted a pestle, well-worn and heavy. Another time he found a tiny harbour seal, a talisman that fit perfectly into the palm of a hand. These were relics of the Homalco Indigenous people who have lived in the area for millennia.

When Dad first began working in the woods, he got a job in Toba Inlet. As he was eating lunch one day, he leaned back on a mossy log, and looking up, he saw that it swept skyward into the prow of a canoe, a vision of decaying beauty. The hull was unfinished, perhaps abandoned when the carvers realized the grain of the wood was not straight enough to take the precise lines of a dugout. I often thought about that ghostly monument softening back into the soil, and I asked Dad to take me to see it, but he said he couldn't remember exactly where it was. It was so long ago.

The day he noticed the markings on the cliffs, he and Mum weren't exactly sure what they were looking at. The trees at the base of the cliff had grown up around the images, blocking a clear view. He had to get a closer look. Tying the boat to a tree on the shoreline, he began to climb the rock face while Mum remained in the boat, shouting up to him, "Don't do anything stupid," even though that's exactly what he was doing.

Every few minutes, cascades of pebbles tumbled into the water as he traversed the cliffs, climbing from one ledge to the next, grabbing onto tree branches for support. Then, silence. Mum called up to him again, but he didn't answer. After about an hour, he was back at the base of the cliff, eager to tell Mum, "You aren't going to believe what's up there." He described paintings (pictographs) running along the cliff face in a ribbon of figures resembling humans, but he wasn't sure, and below the figures, there were burial boxes hanging in the trees and bits of woven cedar blanket on the ground, fallen there over time. That night, our family made a pact not to tell anybody about the site, though we were confident it was well known to the Homalco people and had probably been "discovered" by other white people years before. We just didn't want anybody snooping around with wise ideas about removing anything and putting it on display.

A few days before my father died, a dugout canoe drifted into the cove below my parents' home on the Sunshine Coast. It was small, only big enough for one person and barely seaworthy after floating around the coast for years. Mum contacted the nearby shíshálh Nation and two men came by, loaded the canoe into the back of a pickup and drove off, taking it back home.

My father at the end of another very long day.

Rained to Beat Hell

NOT LONG AGO, I FOUND MY FATHER'S WORK DIARY FROM 1959, shortly after he and Uncle Kurt had established their camp in Orford Bay. It's a high-school notebook, the kind with ruled paper and a wire spine, and it has the company name, Willcock & Wankel Logging Ltd., scrawled across the front cover in Dad's grade-school handwriting. The back cover is marked up with dozens of calculations, and it is easy to guess that my father was adding up the number of logs sold against the company's expenses, trying to predict whether or not he and Uncle Kurt could stay in business one more year.

Inside the notebook, I found a scrap of paper on which he had written, "I worked so much because I wanted to put some money aside for Joan and the girls in case I got killed in the woods." He must have added this note to the diary shortly before he died. My parents were big on notes. They left them all over the place: in drawers, between the pages of books, and taped to the back of pictures. This was their way of making sure that when they were gone, my sisters and I could attach meaning to the things they left behind.

The diary spans one logging season, from early March, when the weather was good enough to begin working in the woods, and runs through until the end of November, when camp shut down for the winter. It's an account of how many loads of logs were hauled to the ocean each day and a record of the bad weather and breakdowns that made the work so damn hard. This was logging. Each load of logs contributed to paying the crew's wages, covering expenses, and giving loggers a few weeks off each year to go home to their families.

My father's record of the last three weeks in November are brief and to the point. He and Uncle Kurt and the rest of the crew must have been exhausted. They were hauling logs seven days a week, trying to get as many as possible into a boom and towed to Vancouver before winter set in.

Nov 10—rained to beat hell, flat tire, 3 loads

Nov 11—road washed out in several places, had to quit hauling, no loads, repaired tires after dinner

Nov 12—finished repairing washout, cook quit

Nov 13—mechanic flew in from Campbell River to work on truck transmission, lost 1.5 hours

Nov 14—hauled all day, 8 loads

Nov 15—rained to beat hell, 7 loads

Nov 16—rained all day, road washed out in several places, had to quit hauling, 4 loads

Nov 17—worked on the road, 2 flat tires, no logs

Nov 18—5 loads

Nov 19—transmission on truck haywire, 5 loads

Nov 20—transmission broke down, 2 loads, Floyd made lemon meringue pie, not so good

Nov 21—worked on transmission, no logs

Nov 22—rained to beat hell, 5 loads

Nov 23—snowed, 3 loads

Nov 24—no work, fixed brakes on truck

Nov 25—snowed to beat hell, 4 loads

Nov 2—flat tires all day, no loads

Nov 27—Kurt pushed snow off road, 3 loads

Nov 28—poured rain all afternoon, logs ready to go to Vancouver
Nov 29—crew flew out, Kurt and I closed up camp
Nov 30—watchman flew in
Dec 1—Kurt and I flew out
Total loads this year 401

There would be enough money to keep going one more year.

Thank Youse

To begin I would like to thank my parents who were brave and hard-working and honest and in many ways gave me and my sisters the kind of childhood I wish all children could have. I'd also especially like to thank my sister Wendy who has a better memory than I do and has been very helpful in filling in the blanks of things I had long forgotten. I value her sense of humour, which is almost as good as mine, and I applaud her for trying to keep up. And my brother-in-law, Ken, one of the first readers of *Up The Coast* who laughed when he read the book, and that meant everything.

Also, I was very lucky to have had my friend and talented artist, Elizabeth Sutherland-Cox generously provide her watercolour painting for the cover of the book. She is also a woman of the coast and understands what that means in every sense.

And, Sandra Anderson, my editor. I was blessed. She patiently, professionally, and kindly guided me along the way, never losing her enthusiasm for the manuscript. It was also a pleasure to exchange Netflix suggestions with her during the pandemic. And I would like to take this opportunity to apologize for the thousands of commas she deleted from the manuscript without a single complaint. Thank you so much.

I am also grateful for the steady guidance and support of Claire Kelly and Matt Bowes at NeWest Press who managed the entire process of taking *Up The Coast* from manuscript to bookstores. I appreciate their patience and hard work.

I am also eternally grateful to Joanne and Ruby and Ting. You know why. You are simply the best.

And lastly, to my husband, Geoff who never stopped providing technical support and buckets of ink and toner and steady encouragement.

Kathryn Willcock was born in Vancouver and spent her early years in logging camps on the coast of B.C., particularly Bute Inlet where she and her sisters spent their days playing on the banks of the Orford River, an area considered one of the world's best locations for viewing grizzly bear.